The Diamond Anointing

When the Pressures & Processes of Life Propel you into Greatness

By

Sharon D. "Skyy" Chase

©Copyright 2018 – The Diamond Anointing by
Sharon D. "Skyy" Chase

All Rights Reserved. This book is protected by the copyright laws of the United States of America. This book may not be copied or reprinted for commercial gain or profit. Permission will be granted upon request. Unless otherwise identified Scripture, quotations are taken from The King James Version.

ISBN: -13: 978-1727632705
ISBN: - 10: 1727632702

Acknowledgements

I would like to acknowledge my children Devine, Dante, Chiffon, and Aniya, they are my inspiration for everything that I do. I could not have asked for more brilliant children, this book is a part of my earthy legacy; I have already left them a spiritual legacy. I have taught them what I know about God, it was important for me to teach them how to hear from God and to have their own relationship with him, because when you stand before the Throne, and we all will, Momma will not be there, you must know God for yourself.

God has let me know, that I have passed the test where my children are concerned and that he is well pleased. I wanted to write a book not only to leave for my children but one that would help people to overcome and understand that truly, everything is working out for your good. It is all relative, but more importantly, I wanted to write a book that my children could not only read but be proud of. So, this is for you guys, you all have been my inspiration, my motivation. Thank you for being who you have become.

I want to give a special acknowledgement to my cousin, Ngozi Thomas, she pushed me to write this book, she could not understand how I made it out, still clothed in my righteous mind. It took some time for me to figure it out, but with much prayer. I decided it was not all in vain and if my story could help anyone then it was all worth it.

I want to thank my mentor Thyra Jones, who I thought I met by accident, but we know there is no such thing. She is the definition of "Go the Extra Mile", everything I know about earthly evangelism, I learned from her. Thank you for always being you.

I want to thank my auntie, Camiller Thomas, who is now deceased; she taught me that education was priceless; she gave me a sense of style and travel. She opened my eyes to the possibilities of life. It is because of her that my library has over fifteen - hundred books and counting. Love you auntie miss you much.

I would be remiss if I did not thank my grandmother, Mae Campbell, who is also deceased. Because of her, I am the woman I am today; she taught me all the social graces. She taught me how to be a lady and how to carry myself. She was determined that just because I lived in the projects did not mean the projects had to live in me, she taught me diversity and never try to fit in where you don't belong. She taught me self-esteem and self-acceptance at an early age, because of her I embrace my uniqueness. She taught me how to uniquely be me. She was my protector, my educator, and my friend. I miss her telling me awesome stories; she made you feel as if you were there. She taught me humanitarianism and to always look out for your fellow man because looking out for him meant you were looking out for yourself.

Last but not least my only brother, Roland D. Warren and my mother, Dorothy L. Terry, who are both deceased, sometimes people are not in your life to teach you what to do, but what not to do. You can learn from the mistakes of someone else's life without having to make your own.

I pray that this book blesses you and leaves an indelible mark on your heart of hope, faith, and belief, that dreams really do come true. **DREAMS ONLY WORK IF YOU DO!**

JEREMIAH 17:1

The sin of Judah is written with a pen of iron, and with the point of a Diamond: it is graven upon the table of their heart and upon the horns of your altars

A pen of iron - an iron chisel for cutting inscriptions upon tables of stone.
The point of a diamond - The ancients were well acquainted with the cutting powers of the diamond.

Diamond – a precious stone consisting of a clear and colorless crystalline form of pure carbon, the hardest naturally occurring substance

Anointing – special ability rubbed on you by God to accomplish a special assignment, grace

I pray that this book will leave a deep mark an ineradicable scar; tattooed on your heart and mind written with a stylus of an iron pen with the tip of a diamond. Let the words of this book burn in the hearts of men with the conviction that ignites the fire of transformation, reformation that will change laws, policies, and ordinances to reflect equality for all of humankind.

Sharon D. "Skyy" Chase

TABLE OF CONTENTS

SECTION I THE PROCESS 1
    1. WHY–NOT WHY ME-JUST WHY 1
    2. THE MAKING OF A DIAMOND 3
    3. CLARITY 6
    4. CUT 11
    5. COLOR 16
    6. CARAT 24
    7. AUTHENTICITY 35

SECTION II DEFINING & ANALYZING THE PROBLEM ... 38
    8. REDEFINING POVERTY 38
    9. DEAR MR PRESIDENT 49
    10. PROPOSAL FOR CHANGE 59

SECTION III PRODUCTIVE SOLUTIONS 65
    11. CHANGE YOUR MIND–IT'S YOUR PEROGATIVE 65
    12. MAKE FRIENDS WITH MONEY 70
    13. AFFIRMATIONS–YOU ARE WORTH IT 79

TRADEMARK PROGRAMS TO ASSIST YOU IN YOUR

JOURNEY TO GREATNESS

PURPOSE & IDENTITYPATH™ 85

COMPANY OF MEN BOOK CLUB REVIEW© 86

STEPS™ (STRATEGIES TO ELEVATE OUT OF POVERTY SUCCESSFULLY) 87

POSSESS YOUR GATES™ 88

#WRITEYOURWAYTOMILLIONS 91

RESOURCES 95

Why-Not Why Me-Just Why?

The definition of Why: for what; for what reason, cause or purpose.

When I was a little girl going to church with my grandmother, we grew up in a Pentecostal background; it was such a fun time. There were so many things going on that I did not understand, I have always had a knowing and insight into things and people, but the church was a place of wonder. I have a very inquisitive mind, I always wanted to know how things worked. I would later find out that I have a very scientific way of seeing things. So **WHY** was my favorite question to Ask.

Heaven would always oblige me and give me the answer as to Why something was or was not. I remember at the age of eight, we had a program at church and all of the children had a passage of scripture to memorize, mine was Ecclesiastes 3, the entire chapter, to everything there is a season, to this day I still remember this scripture it never left me, it would become the mantra of my life, these words have carried me and caused me to have incredible insight into the seasons, times, and synchronicity of my life and others.

I was told never to question God, I remember thinking why wouldn't you question the one who has all the answers? Well, I did not listen to that bad advice. Everything I have ever gotten, every mystery of life unlocked, it was because I asked God **WHY?**

This book was birthed because growing up in Philadelphia Diamond Street, walking home from Strawberry Mansion Jr. Sr. High School it was nine blocks away on the corner of 32nd Susquehanna & Dauphin (yes, I grew up on Diamond Street, God does have a sense of humor)

I would walk past drug dealers on the corners, condemned abandoned brownstones with beautiful architecture, skid row bums begging for change, standing in front of the liquor store. I would see the same people sitting on the brick row homes on the steps being nosy, I would speak to my elders doing nothing every single day. Can you imagine living among adults where nobody had a job, everyone was on some type of government assistance, where is the role model in that?

I would ask God every day WHY? Why do I live here? Why did they stack these people together like sardines on top of each other? Why do they call this the projects, a project means it has a beginning and an end? When will this drama end? Why do you want me to see and witness, murder, rape, shootings, killings, fighting, and drugs every day? Why do you have me here?

So, for every time I asked God WHY –this book is the answer he gave me. Because you are my **DIAMOND.** Yes, God can talk, I did not know what it meant to be a Diamond, because I was at the beginning stages of the process. Because I asked Why, I began to get clarity and understanding of things that I witnessed. I was in the valley of the shadow of death. Just like Diamonds start out in a dark place, as a lump of black coal, they go through a rigorous process, they are graded, weighed and cut, to reveal its natural brilliance, then it is displayed for all to see from obscurity to opulence.

The Making of a Diamond

According to Webster's Dictionary, the definition of a jewel is "a precious stone, typically a single crystal or a cut and polished piece of a lustrous or translucent mineral." The ancient Greeks believed that diamonds were splinters of stars fallen to earth. The word diamond in the Greek language translates as "Adamas" which means unconquerable and indestructible. The diamond is the hardest of all gemstones known to man. It is also the simplest in composition and is made up of only one element—common carbon.

Diamonds are carried to the surface of the earth by volcanic eruptions; only very few diamonds survive the hazardous journey from the depths of the earth to reach the surface. Diamonds are brittle; if hit hard with a hammer, a diamond will shatter or splinter. Even though a diamond can be broken, a diamond seemingly lasts forever. God is forming His jewels. The jeweler will tell you it is all about the 5 C's: carat, cut, color, clarity, and certificate of authenticity, which dictate the price, grade, and value, which determines the diamonds worth.

Did you know that God refers to His people as precious jewels? In Malachi 3:17 God declares, "They shall be Mine," says the Lord of hosts, "On the day that I make them my jewels." God is referring to—

those written in the Book of Remembrance. The manner in which God lets us know He wants to possess us is so intimate, loving, and beautiful.

A diamond does not start out polished and shining but with enough pressure and time, it becomes spectacular and brilliant.

When we are going through the trials of life, we do not think that it is by design, we often think this is the way my life is supposed to be. Life gave me lemons, so I will make lemonade. Living one day at a time, but never looking at the bigger picture at hand, that we all are here for a reason, season, purpose, and time.

When you are in the darkness, a lump of coal buried deep inside an environment of death, chaos, and destruction, survival becomes the order of the day.

When does a diamond become a diamond, when it's in the dark or when it is brought to the light? A diamond becomes a diamond at the moment of existence. The lump of coal undiscovered in the cave makes it no less a diamond, in other words, your present situation, circumstance does not define your purpose. Growing up in Diamond Street projects, I would have never thought in a million years that my life was going through a process, for me to reach the maximum height of my brilliance, so my light could shine to one day, free other people. I just wanted to make it through the valley of the shadow of death, death and more death. My life is not my own, I was allowed to walk through the valley so that you could know that, you can make it out, so that when you yield to the process, the brilliance of your light, will bring so much clarity to your life, you can see your way clear to live the life of your destiny. Your life is not relegated or defined by the government, your traumas, hurts, situation or the circumference in which you find yourself. Adversity is not the enemy, little did I know that *"Adversity is the diamond dust that Heaven polishes its jewels with,"* Thomas Carlyle. The darkness is only temporary, but it is also necessary, "Darkness cannot drive out darkness, only light can do that.", Dr. Martin Luther King. You must shine bright like a diamond, as a beacon of light stepping out of the cave of despair, into the possibility and purpose of your life. When you find yourself in darkness, this is the beginning of the process, not the end. It is the Making of a Diamond.

Clarity-New Sight, Greater Understanding

Diamond Clarity is a combination of how many inclusions occur within a diamond and how noticeable they are. Most diamonds contain blemishes on the outside of the diamond or inclusions trapped inside the diamond. These inclusions are what distinguish a single diamond from every other diamond. The very things we see as flaws are what makes you distinct and different. Your greatness is what makes you different, but instead of embracing it, we reject that part of ourselves.

Many of us wrestle with the feelings of inadequacies and our weaknesses, between who we are and who we are meant to be. We feel unqualified to live out the calling we imagine. But the blemishes blind us to the truth that we still carry value and our life can still be used for good. We become too caught up in our situation that we can't see the forest for the trees. Every diamond has a flaw, blemish or an inclusion, it is given a grade, it still has value and can be sold. When diamonds are mined they are preserved in their natural state, meaning they are not changed.

Clarity comes when we can see the truth about who we are and who we can become. We must accept that because we are flawed, it does not disqualify you from the destiny awaiting you. We lack clarity because we are focusing on our weaknesses and our blemishes, instead of embracing ourselves in totality, flaws and all, it is these blemishes that make us unique. Embrace your big nose, your foot that is smaller than the other, your eyes that are a little crossed, all of those imperfections make you who you are. Clarity came to me in the second grade when we first moved to Diamond Street projects. Being black was not an easy thing to be and the world was a constant reminder that you were flawed, ugly, rejected and simply not qualified. I will never forget my teacher, Miss Asbury, she was fair-skinned beautiful with a headful of beautiful hair, that she wore in the biggest, roundest afro I had ever seen, and it was gleaming and glistening, she would come to school with her Dashiki on she was proud to be a black woman. She taught us to be proud of our culture and who we are, she would teach us about our culture and our heritage and how we came from Kings & Queens. She would teach us about all the inventions, how smart, brilliant we were as a culture of people and that we started civilization. My self-esteem went through the roof, this was amazing, I was somebody, I always knew I was born to do great things in the world. I was so proud to learn all of this information about myself, something was coming alive in me. She truly changed my life, I could accept myself flaws and all because I belonged to a rich heritage and history. The activist was awakened in me which started me on the path of advocacy. The advocate that I was one day destined to become. I never liked the injustice of any kind toward any people but if I was going to fight for anyone it would first be my own people. Clarity came and gave me new insight and a greater understanding that my life had meaning, and that I could truly make a difference in someone's life. I was in the second grade, but I have always been ahead of my time. I gained incredible clarity and insight into who I was, society tells us to hide our weaknesses and that the secret to success is to appear flawless. The diamond still shines with its inclusions and blemishes, you see the true essence of the beauty it possesses. We must embrace that we are flawed and that in spite of that, it does not disqualify us but distinguishes us and makes us uniquely who we are, right now.

We all have dealt with feelings of insecurity, unworthiness, and self-doubt, this is part of the process. Growing up, I battled with shame and humiliation, living in filth, this has a profound effect on your mental health. My elementary school was located right next to the projects, there were eight buildings with twelve floors. not counting the ground floor, each floor had eight apartments, you do the math.

It felt like you were living in a war zone, (no disrespect to our Vets) it became normal to hear about or read about the dead bodies of little children who had been raped, killed and thrown into a heap of trash behind the building for someone to discover accidentally on their way to school. Or to smell a body being burned in the incinerator, each building had a janitor, but they only burned the trash once a week, when you smell a dead body you never forget that smell.

I know what it's like to feel unworthy because you are looked down upon because your parents have no money, and society has placed you in this container I call **POVERTY** and made you feel like you were nothing and no one, but I remember my teacher causing the light bulb to go off in my head, clarity was the tool she gave us that day, she gave us a new perspective and a different way of looking at our circumstances, she gave us hope to go on another day. Clarity also allows you to build your critical thinking skills because as the years go by, the dysfunction becomes a way of life, you begin to think that the way you live is normal. Clarity caused me to see myself different, I accepted me for me, and I got rid of the definition that someone had placed on me. Although I was surrounded by constant pressure, that day was a breakthrough for me and it would change my life forever. I learned how to be comfortable in my own skin, no longer would I be distracted by external things that cause me to lose sight of what really mattered. I have held true to this even as an adult, my grandmother would always say to me long before Jessie Jackson gave his speech," just because you live in the projects, it doesn't mean the projects have to live in you." "I hold this truth to be self-evident that all men are created **EQUAL:** –in the words of the late great Dr. Martin Luther King. You and I are not less than, where you live does not define you or disqualify you, you were born to make manifest the glory of God and to shine bright like a **DIAMOND.** This poem quoted in Nelson Mandela's Inaugural Speech, 1994.

Marianne Williamson

Return to Love

Our deepest fear is not that we are inadequate.
Our deepest fear in that we are powerful beyond
measure. It is our Light, not our Darkness that most
frightens us.
We ask ourselves, who am I to be brilliant, gorgeous, talented, fabulous?
Actually, who are you not to be?

You are a child of God. Your playing small does not serve the World.

There is nothing enlightening about shrinking so that other people won't feel unsure around you. We were born to make manifest the glory of God that is within us. It is not just in some of us; it is in everyone. As we let our own Light shine, we consciously give other people permission to do the same.

As we are liberated from our own fear, our presence automatically liberates others."

Cut-Wounded, Healed Without Scars

A Diamonds cut is perhaps the most important of the five Cs, so it is important to understand how this quality affects the properties and values of a diamond. A good cut gives a diamond its brilliance, which is that brightness that seems to come from the very heart of a diamond. The angles and finish of any diamond are what determine its ability to handle light, which leads to brilliance.

I could get very deep with this and talk about grade, shape, height, but I want to keep it simple so that the significance of this process is not lost. In this parallel, I want to come from the perspective of wounds, traumas and hurts. These are the types of cuts you endure when you grow up in the container I call **POVERTY.** It would seem pretty cruel to imply that God wants you to be cut, God makes the best of every situation, He wastes nothing and uses everything so that what you went through was not in vain, often time we blame God for things in which he has nothing to do with. Every life has value in God's eyes, when you are a child you become a product of the decisions of your parents, I would soon learn that everything in life has a duality, to be cut is to allow what is precious and valuable on the inside to be seen on the outside. To be cut is to know pain and pain leads to change. The cuts that I endured was to my psyche. As I grew older, I wondered why none of the adults ever talked about escaping this thing called **POVERTY**, I grew to hate **POVERTY,** it was like a disease that would not go away. I did not know that you have control, I wanted to erase it from everyone's life, it was like a cancer that ate away at your soul every day. My mother was engrossed in the life cycle of **POVERTY**, and despair, she drank and did drugs to escape the pain of her life. It was as if all of the adults came into an invisible agreement with **POVERTY**, they did not question it, they did not fight it, they just accepted it. Poverty was the doorkeeper to a whole host of other things, I witnessed my mother being raped, that cut me to my core, one boyfriend she had stabbed her over twenty- times within inches of her life. I would have to break up fights because her boyfriend would beat, punch, stomp, kick and drag her like she was a dog, these men were violent savages who took all of their rage, frustration, and wrath out on the women and children in their lives. Living in poverty creates an anger that spews out like hot molten lava embedded within a person from years of hopelessness, despair, discouragement, and disappointment, not to make excuses, but these are the effects that living years of oppression will lead to not to mention suicide, homicide, and chronic depression. Most people who grow up in these adverse conditions are severely depressed. They hurt because they feel no one cares, they are in a forgotten place among a forgotten people. I am here to tell you that you are not forgotten, you must be made aware that greatness is made in the furnace of great affliction.

When a son is born he is cut to circumcise him, it is the most painful cut you can see your baby go through but it protecting him from infections. Because in his loins he carries a generation, seeds of future greatness. The circumcision of your heart, cutting out your hard heart and giving you a heart of compassion, empathy, sympathy for your fellow man. You may find yourself in what seems like an impossible situation and you feel lost and cursed. The cutting is for your own good, to reveal the true you.

It reminds me of a documentary I watched that ripped my heart to shreds, "The Kalief Browder", story, he was falsely accused and sat in prison for three years, while he proclaimed his innocence, this young man was cut beyond belief, but inside of him was a brilliant mind and a heart of pure gold. His life was sacrificed and martyred so that his story could be exposed to the world, the injustice of the Industrial Prison Complex, he endured his cuts like a good soldier, one might say, where was God, he was there giving him the strength, perseverance, endurance to stand in the face of tremendous cutting. He was wounded for our transgressions, he was bruised for our iniquities, in order to reign there is a suffering that takes place. You must recognize that what you are facing is only temporary, just for a moment, but carries with it a greater weight of purpose. Your suffering is not in vain, every step you take on this journey called life is leading you to a place of purpose and your final destination.

Growing up in the projects was like a living hell, surely there has to be more to life. On this battleground, you are being sharpened your discernment is exercised daily, your ability to recognize people, places, things are all being developed, it serves as your protection, the cuttings saving your very life. But because we are not aware of our destiny and purpose, life is lived haphazardly, dangerously and recklessly. I know it is difficult, it feels unfair, all of these people are making decisions that affect and infect your life and you feel lost in the wind. This is not the way your life was intended to be, but because you are here it will all work out for your benefit. Do not allow the hurt to hold you back, forgiveness is key, because you will be cut by the people who are close to you, but betrayal is a character in this life and will indeed rear its ugly head. Human beings were not designed to live with emotional or psychological pain for indefinite periods of time, we must not take the cutting personally. I was treated horribly by my mother, and to this day my children and those around me never understood why I continued to love her to the day she died. I would ask my grandmother, "why does she hate me and make my life a living hell?" I would ask God, "Why did you make her my mother? He made her my mother for where I was going and not for the present moment. I did not realize how much I had learned from my mother watching her life and learning from her mistakes, her life was not in vain because I learned the lessons for her, the ones she missed along the way. God always gives me an answer, he showed me that my mother had mental issues and that she needed love, no matter how she treats you, I want you to love her, forgive her, so I became her protector because she had been beaten all her life. I believe she was bipolar and undiagnosed for many ailments and like many women who grow up in the container of **POVERTY** they see no value in their lives, and they believe that this is how it is supposed to be. The furnace of this negative experience has a different effect on each person, but if you will step outside of the situation and understand that it is not personal but purposeful your endurance level will rise. I understood that my mother did not know how to show me love she could not give me something that she never had, but I loved her then and I love her now. Often times we allow the cutting to make us bitter instead of better. The cutting away of bitterness, unforgiveness, anger, disappointment, and every negative emotion, let it go, let it fall away to reveal the brilliance of the light that is within you. You are priceless and valuable beyond measure. When my mother died I was right by her side, it was a bitter sweet moment, finally she would know peace, I had never seen her be happy, only miserable, I never heard her talk about her dreams, goals, life beat the life out of her, she ended up smoking crack, she succumbed to years of abuse and mistreatment. My heart hurt for her, so when she passed away, I knew finally she could find peace. Letherlifebealessontoyou, that this process is not designed to crush you, but to make you into the masterpiece that you were called to be. Do not allow your bad choices or your parent's bad choices to knock you out of the game.

I would get up early and leave out of the projects, I removed myself from the container, I was a part, but I wasn't apart. I knew I was destined for greater, you are destined for greater, the most expensive diamonds in the world are found deep down in a dark place, do not allow the dark place to engulf you, understand that the light of day always shines, but greatness is birthed in a dark place, you will emerge, to shine brightly to help others see the way. Do not give up on you, people are waiting for you to shine. I call **POVERTY** a container because you can climb out, it is often referred to as crabs in a barrel. Just like fear, it is only an illusion, the container was meant to be cut away to reveal the authentic you. It is always darkest before the dawning of a new day.

Color-The Prism of Life

Diamonds come in all colors of the spectrum. The predominant color you see in a diamond is yellow, which is caused by the trace element nitrogen. Diamonds come in many colors and they are given a grade. I want to come from the aspect of sight, seeing, perspective, when you are in the container I call **POVERTY,** your sight can be greatly affected. When what you see and hear on a daily basis is negative, chaos continually, it will taint your sight. It is important not to allow your environment to mar you. I have always been able to see the invisible, hear what is not spoken, the blackness of the prism is what causes you to see color. Black is the culmination of all colors, look beyond what your natural eyes can see. Seek the true meaning of your circumstance. See the color in your life, its there, its clouded by distraction.

I am an early riser, on the weekends I would get up early, get dressed and leave out of Diamond Street projects. My grandmother never wanted me to live there so every chance he got I was allowed to travel. Most people growing up in the projects never leave out from where they grew up. Life is like a spectrum of color and we need opportunities to experience something other than death, and destruction.

I had a special place where I would go, sometimes I would ride my bike, or walk to Fairmount Park. Philadelphia is a very historical city, it is full of beautiful architecture, murals, and statues. I love to be around water, I loved to write plays, I would go to the park and spend time on this statue called – **The Spirit of Enterprise**, little did I know how significant this would mean to me later in life. I would sit there for hours, planning my life, making decisions about how I wanted my life to be. The statue is a muscular pioneer who surges forward, one hand shading his eyes as he scans the horizon, the other holding a caduceus. Echoing his movement is a great eagle with his wings outstretched. It overlooks the Schuylkill River, and it was the quickest way to get to my grandmother's house. The front of the Statue held an inscription, which I would read every time I would climb on top and sit down to think, reflect and write. It reads – *Our nation, glorious in youth and strength look into the future with fearless and eager eyes as vigorous as a young man to run a race* "Theodore Roosevelt" I did not know that I was being processed to one day be a pioneer, in my life, being one of the first to go to college and get my degree, the first to buy a home, so many firsts, but Philadelphia is a place of first. I spent many years sitting on this statue, it was my secret place and my favorite place in the park. The statue held so much meaning for me, I was very enterprising and entrepreneurial, I always wanted to start my own business, because I was a free spirit. When you grow up in the container I call **POVERTY**, you don't like being confined. Spending time in the park at this statue was a constant reminder, that life had more to offer, there was more on the horizon and I had to go find it, the eagle has the sharpest eyes of any bird, I have always been an eagle, seeing things that no one could see, being a visionary can be a lonely road sometimes. Eagles fly high and they only congregate with other eagles. Those who fly solo develop the strongest wings. I was embracing my color and in doing so, it opened up a new world to me. I had to find ways to keep my mind, if you wake up every day and all you see is filth, dirt, killing, gossip, fighting, screaming, hollering, despair, disdain, you begin to be shaped by your surrounding and poverty would have won. I needed to soar above my situation and my circumstance, I had to experience the prism of life an embrace all the colors. I spent a great deal of time with my aunt and grandmother, it was my aunt who gave me my love of reading. I would sit on this statue and read books, write plays, no one never bothered me there, watching the boats row on the water. I remember my sixth-grade teacher, Mrs. Brinkley, she was my favorite teacher, but she stayed sick a lot because she had sickle cell anemia, she would give us a homework assignment every day to read the paper and bring in a current event, we had to stand in front of the class and explain it. I never liked watching the local news because it was so depressing, just more of the same if I wanted to see a drive-by shooting I could sit in my bedroom window and watch a car drive up and spray the crowd. The local news never appealed to me, I was more interested in what was going on in the world. I would go to the library and read the world news. I watched the world news on TV, and still to this day, I am concerned with all nations, colors, and creeds. Growing up in the project's kids don't really like to read unless they had too. Reading added color to my life, it was also a form of escape for me.

Often, we assume that every difficult situation that comes our way is a test, one meant to stretch us and challenge the very core of our lives. The diamond has many facets, which means there is not just one way to see things. I was allowed to travel because my grandmother wanted me to know, see, and experience that there was more to life than living in the projects. I remember I would go to Pittsburgh with my grandmother's sister Aunt, Mozelle and her daughter Barbara. I loved going to Pittsburgh, Barbara and I would fuss over which sister could cook the best, they both could cook, but I loved my grandmother and I would never vote against her for anyone. My aunt, Mozelle worked in a mansion, a real mansion, she worked for a wealthy couple, who would leave their beautiful home and go on holiday and travel to faraway places. Can you imagine how much color this added to my life? I would run through this house and act like it was mine, it had an Olympic size pool and we would swim and sip on fruity drinks in pretty glasses our aunt would make for us. Barbara was an aspiring actress, so she would act like she was the lady of the house, we would always go into the wine cellar because we knew aunt, Mozelle would have a fit, they had bottles of expensive wines in that cellar, it was huge. We would go to the bathhouse and climb up top and lay on the waterbed that had a sun roof to bask in the sun. How many beautiful memories I had from these experiences, it was a blessing to see how people who had money lived. People with money did not live in a container they had the freedom to travel and do the things their heart desired. So, what makes them so much different than people with no money. Money was not created to define your life or give your life value. Money is only a scoring card that gives value to hard work, talent, time and effort. I learned if I worked hard I could one day have a beautiful life and benefit from the fruits of my labor. God knows the plans he has for each of us, it is our responsibility to find out what that plan is and get to work.

You can rewrite your destiny, you don't have to accept what you have been told about your life, diamonds are not meant to remain in the dark. The purpose of a diamond is to shine and be seen. Diamonds are given different grades for their color, meaning every diamond has a purpose, a place and a position in the crown, the process of making a diamond is so that the potential or power that resides within can been seen on the outside. You were born with potential, goodness, trust and greatness. The character of the diamond is developed in calm but proven in chaos. I want you to take the clarity and new insight and apply it to every situation you are facing and realize, obstacles are not stopping signs, obstacles are meant to be overcome, obstacles are designed to make you stronger, wiser, better, not to remain stuck in the dark place. I recently went horseback riding for my birthday, I am still adding color to my life, trying new things. I learned a few things about horses, when a horse is running on the obstacle course, just before he gets to the obstacle, he has to jump over the hurdle, I wondered, why don't they trip and fall? Horses don't focus on the obstacle directly in front of them for if they do, they will stumble and fall, they focus on the obstacle at the end, because it enables them to clear the hurdle directly in front of them. The horses wear a blinder to keep focused, I am not saying put on blinders to your situation, I am saying do not focus on the negative aspects of the situation, know that you are strong enough, smart enough, to defeat the challenge. God speaks the end from the beginning, focus on the end. For the joy that was set before him, he endured. Keep your focus on the big picture.

You were chosen because you have everything it takes to endure because the race is not given to the swift but to those who endure to the end. We lived in Diamond Street projects from the time I was in the second grade, until I graduated high school, at the age of eighteen, that was a long time to endure, but because I knew that life had more to offer and the process had prepared me for the next phases of my life. I could face life knowing, that if I could make it through this, I could make it through anything. Like, Joseph in the Bible, he was in prison, but he went from prison to the palace. The key to making it out of the pit is to conquer every level. The process is preparing you to accomplish great things in your life, don't forfeit the process. Your dreams, and goals, are at stake, don't die in the wilderness. Don't pitch a tent in the wilderness; your goals are the first step in turning the invisible into the visible. The process is designed to make you not break you. How was I able to make it out, because I have incredible insight, my perspective is God's perspective, he has given me the eyes of the eagle, it was no coincidence I spent years sitting on that statue, it was the culmination of what my life was to become. A pioneer, a forerunner, a trailblazer, a financier, entrepreneur, all of that greatness sitting inside of you, cannot go to waste. Decide today that you will add color to your life, read a book, go to a museum, catch a bus, a plane, fly to another state, go to an open house, preferably a mansion. We often prevent our own deliverance by blocking the healing process. Perhaps, sit is pride that gets in the way, but this is how I made it out, I became impervious to negativity in my surroundings. I did not internalize it, the killings, shootings, fights, I was determined not to allow **POVERTY** to win. I decided sitting in my special place, that I would **ERADICATE, ANNIHILATE** AND **ERASE POVERTY** every chance I got. I declared war on **POVERTY**, I refused to stay inside that container. I stretched my wings and soared every day, I would leave early in the morning and I would not come back until my curfew. This is how they described me growing up, they told my mother, you have a good daughter, she carries herself like a lady when we see her she is either coming or going. I never stayed in my neighborhood, but I learned some very valuable lessons, not to judge people because you never know who they will become.

I remember my mother sold beer, and I would be sitting at the table doing my homework, some of her customers would stay and drink their beer at the table, now didn't I just see this skid row bum begging for change yesterday and today he is at my house sitting at my kitchen table. He struck up a conversation with me, and asked me, "what I was working on, I told him math, which I was having trouble with Geometry. He said, "oh I was good in math in school", he said I love math, well, he got my attention, He said do you mind if I take a look, well, let me tell you this man was a mathematical genius, not only did he help me with my math, but I passed the test. I had turned up my nose at this man, but it taught me a valuable lesson you never know where the process will lead you and who you will meet along the way. I learned to treat everyone with value because the lack of money does not mean you are poor.

The diamond is the hardest gemstone on the planet because it endured the process and made the cut. It is like the Rose that grew in the concrete, the Rose of Sharon is a premiere rose, a rose among roses, it sets the standard for all the other roses, because it can do something the other roses cannot do – grow through concrete. Diamonds are the same way, they set the standard for all the other stones, the pressure does not break it but makes it add color to your life, you're not made to break but to shine and bloom. One of the most prolific rappers, poets, lyrists was born on my earthly birthday June 16, Mr. Tupac Amari Shakur – I will leave you with these words

> *"Did you hear about the rose that grew from a crack in the concrete? Proving nature's laws wrong, it learned to walk without having feet. Funny, it seems to be keeping its dreams; I learned to breathe fresh air. Long live the rose that grew from concrete when no one else even cared."*

> *"we wouldn't ask why a rose that grew from the concrete for having damaged petals, in turn, we would all celebrate its tenacity, we would all love its will to reach the sun, well, we are the roses, this is the concrete and these are my damaged petals, don't ask me why, thank god, and ask me how"*

We are all diamonds, Tupac understood that we are all destined for greatness, in the midst of the storm, he was aware that everything is not the way it appears. Dig deeper, look deep within yourself, there is a treasure hidden in the darkness. He was on the battlefield and saw himself as a Rose pushing through the concrete, not allowing the situation to stop it from blooming, growing, shining. Be determined to shine, the sun does not ask for permission to shine, it just shines.

Carat –The Weight of It All

Diamond carat weight is the measurement of how much a diamond weighs. The Diamond is designed to carry the weight. The capacity to handle the weight is built inside of the diamond, but it must be discovered. Depending on the size of the diamond determines how much weight it can carry.

Each of us is equipped with the capacity to handle, the pressures, problems that life will often throw our way. We often cry and complain when having to deal with the issues of life, because we do not feel that we have been prepared or we are taking it personally. Growing up I was my mother's self-appointed protector, this was the burden that I chose to carry for myself. My mother was beautiful, she was 5 ft. 2in with a petite frame, she had a fair complexion and soft fine hair that was shoulder length, until she cut it all off, and she had a very sensual, sexy walk, that she was famous for, it was natural, but it brought a lot of attention from men and jealousy from the women. Growing up in an environment where a majority of the people has either low self-esteem or no esteem this can be problematic. In order to survive, you must know how to fight, we fought every day. I am the youngest, I only have one brother, and he was raised in the country, so when he came to the city, they picked on him and teased him, so now I am responsible to protect two people. I had a great relationship with my uncle, he taught me how to box, because just like my mother, I was also very attractive, I had a head full of beautiful hair, also small and petite and I dressed very stylish or as they would call it, I was fly. I recall a major fight in the seventh grade, her name was Jackie Westbrook, and she wanted to fight me because in gym class the teacher told us to stand behind the line and my foot unknowingly was on the line. She decided to call me out after school, she and a crowd of girls followed me home. People did not fight fair, girls carried razorblades under their tongues because if you were pretty they would cut up your face, so when you got into a fight it was to the death and for your life, so you had to pick your fights carefully. So, my uncle decided I was too pretty for my face to be cut up, so he taught me how to box, most girls do not know how to box. I had three strategic moves because I am left handed, south paw, you don't seem my uppercut coming. He taught me that if you hit someone in the chin with enough force and power, no matter how big, you can knock them out. Next move he taught me was, sidestep, most girls put their head down and come at you windmills tyle, he showed me how to sidestep an uppercut to the face. He taught me strategic places to hit people, mainly the esophagus and the temple to constrict blood flow to the brain, which can result in death. It's just that serious.

The first day of school I did not want to fight, so my brother told my mother, that I let her push me and I didn't fight back. My mother said," if you don't fight her, you will have to fight me," so the next day, she and the crowd followed me again, I looked over and my brother was there watching, he said," I got your back. I fought her and of course, she pulled my hair, that is a no, no. I could hear my grandmothers voice saying, "if you bite a person, they lose their strength." I looked up and the only thing I saw was her jaw, so I latched on to her jaw with my teeth with the tenacity of a pit bull and just like my grandmother said. She went limped and the only thing that was keeping her from falling to the ground was my teeth latched on to her jaw. I let her go, she fell to the ground and I stomped her until I saw blood.

Now, this may sound savage, but you have to fight for your life or you will be picked on everyday by everybody. Themediaonlyreportsabout the male gangs, but in the projects, there are female gangs as well, and in order for you not to be a part of a gang, you must fight and beat up all of the members because if not, they will stalk you daily. This is where my boxing skills came in handy, I beat every single girl in the gang, after that I had a reputation, and no one bothered me. I did not even fight girls my own age anymore, I fought my mother's grown friends, one in particular, Miss Candy, she was so jealous of my mother, Miss Candy was the opposite of my mother, she had a horrible shape, double DD, big breast and a flat behind, her sister walked with a limp, they were bullies, they terrorized everyone, but one thing you cannot be is afraid. I have always been quiet, fearless and bold, people usually underestimate me because I do not talk a lot. My grandmother taught me, the loudest one in the room is normally the weaker stone, you don't see me coming. I never understood why my mother was friends with Miss Candy, knowing she was jealous of her, this one day her and my mom were arguing, probably over a man, she was outside loud talking my mom telling her to come outside. I went over to the window and looked out to see what all the commotion was about, and she called me out, she had a reputation for being bad and beating people up, she had two ugly daughters. I said mom, we have to go out there and fight them because if we don't this will not stop. We went outside, I always wore a t-shirt with some kind of saying on it, my jeans, my white high-top converses and my hair in a ponytail. We went outside, all of her family was with her, she was sitting on one side of the bench and my mom sat on the other side, I stood up. I was small, but I was quick and very aware of my surroundings because if they couldn't beat you they would jump you, I carried a box cutter and I would use it. I normally never had to pull a weapon because I would knock you smooth out before you could get close enough to cut me. She was talking trash, showboating, my grandmother always told me if you're going to fight, don't argue, just get to work. I was tired of hearing her mouth, so while she was talking I walked behind her and busted her in the head with a Coca-Cola bottle and blood started flowing down her face, she never saw me coming. I whipped out this dog chain I carried that was metal and started to whip her slow behind, her daughters ran over toward me to jump me and I started whipping them with the dog chain, the police came and took her whole family to jail.

Fight! Fight!! Fight!!! I had to fight my mother's boyfriend because a lot of my friends were raped repeatedly by these predatory men. Unfortunately, rapists are everywhere in the projects, fresh out of Graterford State Prison, most of them. I was mean, I would fight a grizzly bear. I was being tormented by this man, he would make me cook for him, wash his clothes, and if I refused, he would tell lies on me. I remember the day he came into my mother's life, we were sitting outside, in the summer it gets hot in the apartments, we did not have air conditioning, so we would go sit outside, I would not allow my mother to go alone, I would go with her as her protector. I saw a man run from the adjacent building, he sat on the bench where we were sitting, the next thing you know he starts talking to my mother and before the week was out, he had moved into our apartment. I knew something was wrong, all my bells and whistles starting going off, I let him know that I did not like him from day one. I found out that he was on the run, he had been going around raping young girls in the neighborhood. I could not believe I was living with a rapist, so when I told my grandmother she was livid, she gave me instructions as to what to do, if he tried to do anything to me, she told me to throw hot scalding water on him. This one particular day, he and my mom had gotten into an argument and she told him to leave, on Saturdays, I had a routine. I would get up early and go into town and do some shopping, buy me another pair of jeans, Sergio Valente, Baronelli's or Jordache jeans was my favorite, I would go to the fish market and buy some fresh fish, then I would go home, cook breakfast of fish and grits, watch Dr. Shock double feature, then take my boom box and leave out the PJ's until curfew. Well here he comes disrupting my routine, he and my mom were arguing, I was in the kitchen frying fish and making grits, he was really upsetting my mom. I walked over to him standing in the doorway with no shirt on, she was repeatedly asking him to leave, my program is about to come on and I want to hear, because I love horror movies and Dr. Shock was my favorite. He told me to mind my business I am talking to your mother, well I could see that my mother was about to have a nervous breakdown, she was already taking pills for her nerves. I had already put the water for the grits on the stove, I just walked over and put some salt into the water, meanwhile, he is still harassing my mom and now he is beefing at me, I said you have been standing in the door for almost an hour, she said you can't come in, Dr. Shock will be on in about twenty minutes, you are being loud and rude, next thing you know, I walked over to the pot and threw the hot water on him. He sustained third degree burns all over his neck, chest, and arms, he started running around screaming he was on fire, I pushed him out of the door, sat down, ate my breakfast and watched Dr. Shock double feature. This is a true story, I threw the water over my shoulder, I didn't get not one drop on me, the whole pot went on him. I had a bad temper, I hated repeating myself, if I told you once, you better take heed, because I would hurt you really bad. My grandmother found out and asked me, what did he do to you? I told her it was a buildup of being tormented by him over the weeks, I told her that I had found out that he was raping girls, and I did not feel safe around him, and that we only have one T.V and I didn't want to miss Dr. Shock. Everybody thought I was crazy because I showed no remorse, just pure hatred.

Before the year was over, he would be shot in broad daylight, and I was glad because he was the only person I have ever hated in my life. I was changing, the weight of the constant fighting, killing, noise was getting to me, so my grandmother told me to come stay with her for the summer.

I know it seems unbearable, I know, but it will yield a greater weight of glory, I know you are surrounded by lions, tigers, and bears, in that jungle, but if you stay focused and realize, this furnace of affliction is only for a moment, what seems like eternity, it will yield a greater weight of good in your life. You can make it, you were not born to break but to manifest the light that will shine brightly from within you. At that time, I did not realize it was a testing, because I was placed in a jungle, and I had to not only survive but one day to thrive. He had succumbed to his lower nature and instead of being a protector of women, he became a predator of women, his circumstance had turned him into an animal. I did not see a man, I saw an animal, he would beat my mother, I would have to break up the fight, she was walking around with busted lips and black eyes, her beauty was being beaten out of her because we lived among savages. I refused to let **POVERTY**, the PJ's, the people, lack of money win, I was greater, and I knew I was destined to do something great in this world, and so are you. Why am I telling you this, because as an adult I gave my life to God, and what did he do, he used that anger that came out of me, turned it into power and made me a Powerful Prayer Warrior, I just changed battlefields. Whatever weight you are carrying whether real or imagined, assigned or self-appointed. You were built to carry the weight of it, I was fighting people, not in my weight class, but I stepped up to the challenge. because I was born to do it, born to conquer, born to win, born to be a champion. This was my boot camp growing up in the dark causes your spiritual eyes to be sharp, it exercised my discernment and to this day, I can see through people, it sharpened my spiritual senses. Do not allow the weight of the environment to crush you, grapes must be stomped on to get the precious wine out of them. Diamonds must be put through tremendous pressure before the brilliance of the light can emerge. Stop looking externally and realize that there is a valuable treasure deep on the inside of you and your present burden is causing it to bubble up to the top.

No one bothered me, my mother or brother anymore, Jackie Westbrook brought me candy to school every day trying to be my friend. I became a hero to people and to this day people when they are in trouble or need an answer to a problem or situation, they call on me, it was this discovery that caused me to start my own business, because I was always advocating or fighting for someone, in some shape or form. People have always gravitated toward me for answers, I am an introvert, I am quiet and observant, I don't crave attention. But they saw the greatness that is in me, even when I did not know I had it, you have that same greatness, it is no coincidence that you are in a dark place, diamond miners have to go deep to find diamonds and when they are found, the pressure has to be applied before you see the finished product. I always had a knowing, I knew that I did not belong there, you don't belong there, so I submitted to a process that I did not understand, but I refused to let **POVERTY** have the final say. I will fight until I win, when I step into the ring it's because in my mind I have already won. I am a winner, you are a winner, everyday that you wake up to see another day, thank God because in the PJ's someone dies every day.

Many individuals are depressed and literally crushed by the burdens of everyday life, even when the burden can easily be cast away. We don't have to carry the weight of the world on our shoulders. The weight of one life is enough. I put an undue burden upon myself, but I learned something about myself that day, the advocacy that was awakened in me by my teacher in the second grade was being tested, tried and proven. I was stronger, smarter, braver than I thought I was, I conquered my Goliath, with a dog chain, I gained the respect of my whole community, at the time I did not see it that way, but I knew that in order for me to be left alone, I had to put my skills to use. I won because I saw what they did not see, I saw that I was being made, a diamond is hard, it is the hardest of all the gemstones. Your cuts, wounds, hurts are not supposed to destroy you, it is to reveal who you really are.

You are not who the government says you are, media, or any negative word that has been spoken over you. You are a force to be reckoned with, a mighty man of valor, a warrior princess to stand up for the injustices in the world. I dream of going to Africa and I will but before I go to fight for a nation on another continent, I must first fight for my people right here in America.

I know the weight seems too much to bear, but before David could become King he had to defeat, a lion, a tiger, and a bear- before he conquered his Goliath. Goliath represents a situation that appears too big for you to handle, but every Goliath has an Achilles heel, a weakness, God never puts on us more than we can bear. It is only when you decide to step into the ring and fight everything that is holding you down, that you will truly know how great you were made. David was not only fighting Goliath for him but for all of the people that Goliath would torment, people lived in fear every day. So David showed them not to be afraid, just because Goliath is big, as the saying goes the bigger they are, the harder they fall. For all of my friends who had been raped by their mom's boyfriend without knowing it, I became their hero because they stopped being afraid and started fighting back.

Since I was a teenager, I have been 5ft2 just like my mom since I was thirteen, I weighed exactly 100 lbs. petite, just like my mom. I gave them courage, if she can fight back, surely I can do the same and win, when they heard what happened, they could not believe a grown man was scared of a 15-year-old, all the teenage girls he had raped, he met his match, Then I called the cops on him, I turned him in because he was on the run, and I made sure he knew it was me who called. The police came, knocked on the door looking for him, he ran in my room and hid in the closet, I told the police exactly where he was hiding, and when the police asked me was I the one that called, I looked him dead in his face and said yes, I am the one who called, they took him to jail. In fighting for yourself, you fight for other people, to be free. Winning the fight at school, Jackie Westbrook was a bully, all the kids were scared of her, I did not just win for me, but it was for them too. You can't quit, you can't give up, you must not only fight but you must win. You must win for you, your friends, your family, when you win we all win. The weight of the diamond is innate, inborn, it is natural, some are bigger than others, but the result is the same. You have everything it takes to make it out of your present situation, your testimony may not be as horrific as mine, everyone's journey is not the same, there are some lessons you must learn, you must endure the pressure to establish mastery over it, then can you move on. **David Henry Thoreau**:

If you advance confidently in the direction of your dreams and endeavor to live the life which you imagined, you will meet with a success unexpected in common hours. You will put some things behind, you will pass an invisible boundary, new, and more

Liberal laws will begin to establish themselves around and within you, or the old laws will be expanded, and interpreted in your favor in a more liberal sense, and you will live with the license of a higher order of being.

Be Stronger, than your Excuses

Certificate of Authenticity- Pass the Test

One of the most common techniques to test if a diamond was real or synthetic was to scratch gem against the glass — if the glass is scraped or scratched, the diamond's real. Real recognizes real. This is the C that everyone leaves out, no one wants to be certified, to be a real diamond, you must come with a Certificate of Authenticity; cubic zirconia may look like a diamond, but it has not been processed through. We have a whole lot of people calling themselves Diamonds with no papers. That is a different book, for another time. God qualified me, he did, where are your papers, if he qualified you he would have given you spiritual proof and natural proof because everything has a balance. You may be thinking I have been cut, wounded, bruised, had to fight, conquer Goliaths, now I have to be tested. Yes, you do.

A Certificate of Authenticity, issued by the Gem Certification &Assurance Lab (GCAL), serves as verification of your diamond's quality. Diamond Grading Analysis – This includes the shape, measurements, carat weight, and cut grade based on its proportions, polish, symmetry, color and clarity grades. It also contains any comments regarding the diamond.

Basically, anything that has gone through a process successfully is given a certificate of some kind.

When a baby is born, it is given an APGAR score, Virginia Apgar invented the Apgar score in 1952 as a method to quickly summarize the health of newborn children. Apgar was an anesthesiologist who developed the score in order to ascertain the effects of obstetric anesthesia on babies. Once you pass the test of the APGAR, your mother has to fill out some papers, giving you a name. You are weighed **(carat)**, the umbilical cord is cut **(cut)**, newborn babies don't see in color **(color)**, yet, they only see in black and white, and eventually color, just like the diamond is considered colorless, the hospital gives your mother your birth certificate **(Certificate of Authenticity)** not to validate you, but to certify that you have been processed, from the darkness of your mother's womb into the world. Even Jesus was certified with a birth certificate.

The last C in the process is Care. You are given to your mother to be taken care of, it is all the same process over and over at each stage of your development in life. To summarize it all, your character is being developed, you are purged of all the negativity that tries to destroy, distract, hinder, block, crush, you from being who you were originally called to be, when you emerge you are triumphant, all diamonds don't make the cut.

You have passed the test, now it is time to stretch your wings and soar, you have made it through the worst time in your life. I know a little about flying, I worked as a flight attendant for U.S. Airways before they merged with American Airlines. There are four forces of wind that cause a plane to take off Lift, Drag, Thrust, and Weight, in order to fly above your circumstances, you need all four. When you put it all together, the power that came out of the process, propelling you into your purpose. You have the clarity, confidence and the courage you need to be successful in anything you endeavor to do. It is now time to soar to new heights and move forward.

It is like when a woman is in labor she can experience excruciating pain, but once the baby is given birth too, only joy remains. The pain is forgotten, when I left home I was not angry, I was ready to face the world. I had endured the worst situations imaginable, some people experienced much worse, there are many stories I did not share, I have so many. I just want to deeply express to you that no matter how horrific, hard, unfair, miserable, your life may have been. It was not by chance, that you made it out on the other side. Embrace it, learn from it, use it to make your life better. I came to some life-changing conclusions as a result of what I saw and experienced, I learned many, many lessons that will last me all of my life, I decided most of all that the words of others do not define me. The power of my process proved me, and I came out authentically and uniquely me – as I always say, **"NO ONE CAN BEAT ME AT BEING ME™" and** I love who I am **by S. D. Chase**

"Every test in our life makes us bitter or better, every problem comes to make us or break us."
The choice is ours whether we become victims or victorious.

Section II- Defining & Analyzing the Problem

Redefining (The Word) Poverty

I have always loved words, the meaning, etymology, derivation of words, one day I was reading a letter that was on the table, it was time for my mother to recertify for her apartment, living on someone else's dime gave them the right to be all up in your business. I took notice of the wording on the letter. **Poverty,** so I looked up the definition, it said, penniless, impoverished, insolvent, poverty-stricken, low-income, below, a needy person, vagrant, homeless, down &out, beggar, pauper, derelict, have not, but, in need, hard-up, disadvantaged, bad off, flat broke, strapped, skid row, penurious, suffering from extreme poverty, deficient, totally lacking in money, dirt poor, deprived, disadvantaged, dispossessed, underprivileged, bankrupt, busted, hand-to-mouth, reduced and the list went on. Regardless of what the present situation was saying deep-down inside, I knew I was none of those words. My taste had always been opulent and exquisite, I would go window shopping at my favorite furniture store, Society Hill Furniture, and whatever I liked would always end up being the most expensive in the store. I knew I was destined for wealth, spending summers in the mansion, eating on linen table clothes and fine china at my grandmother's house. I did not care what that letter said I was not poor, period. I watched my mother's life closely to make sure that I would not make the same mistakes she made to end up in such a horrible place in life.

My escape became books and reading, I looked up all the words that were opposite of indigent I was determined not to end up in this place –regardless, despite everything. I stayed positive, I did positive things, I would visit libraries and museums, I made friends with positive people, I became very resourceful. I would go to Love Park and visit the Chamber of Commerce to find out what was going on in the City of Philadelphia. I participated in Walk – a thon's, I would walk for those who could not, the people in my community trusted me and sponsored me to help raise money for those organizations.

My world opened up one day when I was playing softball, our elementary school was right next door, so we would go to the schoolyard and play. I saw some men working, they were moving furniture and throwing things in the trash. I have always been inquisitive, and I was never afraid to talk to perfect strangers. I asked him my favourite question to ask, Why, why are you tearing down what we called the section for retarded kids? No room for political correctness in the hood. He answered and said, "they are bringing in new ones, later I found out that these trailers had asbestos and was making the kids sick. After he left, I went inside, I have always been a loner, and adventurous. I went inside, I saw the teacher's desk, remember those big desks and chairs. I thought I might as well help myself, one man's trash will be my treasure. I never realized how heavy those desks were, what kind of tree did they use to make this puppy? – my mom lived on the third floor, you would think the boys would help me, they saw me pushing this humungous desk, no chivalry in the hood either, survival of the fittest, well at least the elevator was working, my day for a miracle. The elevators are always broken in the

PJ's, we normally walk because it smells horrible, but today I will hold my nose to get this desk to my mom's apartment. I went back and got the teacher's chair. I used the chair to transport all the books, we had a built-in bookcase that went from ceiling to floor, the whole entire wall. I filled it with books that all needed a new home because they would be in the trash if I did not rescue them. I was twelve years old and this was my first library and my place of escape when I was on punishment and couldn't go outside, I would read books. I looked up all the words opposite of poor, and it was one word that erased all the other words, **WEALTHY**–I decided that day I would be that– my first stop would be college, my grandmother taught me that getting a good education was the key to success, learn, feed your brain. The war against **POVERTY** started very young. I always knew that it was an injustice to treat a person as less than because they lacked finances, what does that have to do with me as a person, as a human being? It does not make you superior to me because your bank account has more zeros than mine does. I never agreed with separating people based on bank account, money does not make me or break me. Money is paper, cotton, and ink, we learned that money is used as a valuation system in exchange for goods and services. Money is a tool to be used by me, it does not give me value, it gives value to things, I am more than a thing. In my spirit at a young age, I always had a knowing about things, I knew it was not right. You built these projects because you decided you were better than me because you had more things, who are you to dictate to me and then call me names, well I throw your words back at you and I use my own, Reading books not only helped me to redefine those words but I began to study The Constitution,

Black History, books fed my inquisitiveness and it answered my Why's. I loved reading and I loved school, nothing was keeping me from going to college and pursuing my goal to have my own business. Little did I know that a detour was coming, the business would have to wait. I took the road of work, over the years, I looked at the places I worked as my assignments – the wilderness years. I learned life-changing lessons that I am sharing with you because truly it has caused me to prosper in my business exponentially.

Let's talk about that ugly word **POVERTY** -the federal government has developed a whole system around this word. Let's fast forward to my adulthood and let me share with you my work history. I worked for the Federal Government, in the Human Resource Department, Department of Veterans Affairs; Army Corps of Engineers; City Government, Philadelphia Housing Authority; State Government, Department of Social Services, this was my last assignment before I moved to Houston and finally started my business, What I learned was invaluable, it was all preparing me to step into my greatness.

I received top-notch training, working for the Department of Social Services, I learned policy. I determined eligibility for SNAP (food stamps), Medical and TCA (cash assistance) this is over 15 years of experience. I am a public servant, still advocating, Department of Social Services, I dealt heavily knowing policy and guidelines, to properly determine eligibility to disburse billions of dollars in assistance. Let's talk facts, these are the guidelines passed down in these programs. I wanted to share this because you must read the fine print. This is the container, in order to be eligible, you must be so far below the poverty line, (FPL) Federal Poverty Line, it's designed to keep you in the container. The more policy I learned, I knew this has to be changed. How could the government claim they are fighting Poverty, but sign off on this policy, who is writing these policies? Please Read – Who can live off of this? People who are in dire straits, sign without reading, in order to qualify you must have nothing. I have a ton of work experience, I never stayed on assistance long, but most people don't have my work history, those are the people I am concerned about. These are the working poor, yes you can qualify for assistance and still have a job. People from all walks of life apply and qualify for assistance, many business owners collect assistance. Something is wrong with this picture.

POVERTY GUIDELINE

For families/households with more than 8 persons, add $4,320 for each additional person.

1 $12,140
2 $16,460
3 $20,780
4 $25,100
5 $29,420
6 $33,740
7 $38,060
8 $42,380

These are the guidelines or the container of POVERTY you are placed in, these facts do not have to define you, you can change it. These guidelines are based on policy passed down by the government, this is their definition, do not make it yours.

Working at the Department of Social Services you must know the policy for all three of these programs because thousands of people apply daily. I would sit in the training class and think to myself, that it is a great thing to have programs for when people find themselves in a financial bind, but the more I learned about each program, I saw a pattern, they are designed for you to get on, but to never get off. I am going to give you the advantages of each program so that you can know how to get off and stay off. I will try to keep this as simple as possible because as you can see, the rules are complicated. When I worked at the Department of Social Services, one of the things that I would do is give the clients the real information, there is so much that people do not understand because when you find yourself in a financially challenging situation, you do not stop to read the fine print. Let me use my life as an example, I moved from Philadelphia because my mother died, and my dad was sick, I was born in Washington, D. C but raised in Philadelphia. I had worked at the Philadelphia Housing Authority for ten years, and I was bored and burnt out, I was ready to make a change, so I packed up and moved to Annapolis, the capital of Maryland. I did have a job, I needed a break a reprieve, I just wanted to get my degree, so I went to college working on my associates, in business. I had just sold my home because of financial challenges, (that's a different book) and I wanted to start over, I have the gift of faith, I will pack up and move in a heartbeat without knowing a soul.

So, I graduated from college with an associate degree in Business, I am collecting unemployment, and living on assistance. How did I end up here? (Different Book) Once my unemployment ran out, I needed to find a job but, in the meantime, I figured I would apply to help me over the hump temporarily. I went to the welfare office, I was already receiving food stamps, but I needed some cash, I did not want to apply for cash because the rules are different, and each state disburses their money differently. I had to report to this class each day and submit a report that I was actively looking for a job, I see all kinds of flaws in this plan. I should have been focusing on starting my business at this point, but for some strange reason I had a degree in business but I'm looking to work for someone else, but everything happens for a reason, see how Ecclesiastes is the mantra of my life. I show up and sat in the class and decided, I do not need to be here, not only do I have a high school diploma, I have a degree and by this time over 20 years' worth of work experience. These programs are designed for people who have absolutely nothing, no high school diploma, no work experience, no work history, nothing. I told the lady to listen, I can not come to the class every day, I need a job, she tells me, well you won't be able to receive cash assistance. So she asked, do you have a resume?, I show her my resume and she agrees, she says we have a program that would be perfect for you, The program consists of an eight week training and at the end of the training, if you miss no days, we will hire you for the State of Maryland as a Case Manager, the salary was lower than I was used to but it was a start, I could work my way up.

Lesson 1 – Read your paperwork carefully

Lesson 2 – Utilize your Case Worker

Lesson 3- Ask plenty of questions

I learned a great deal of valuable information working at this job, I knew this was an assignment, but how I would use it to help people started to become clear. The main way that you can get off assistance is to use it to your advantage, as a stepping stone to a better life. This information I am sharing with you, a case manager will not take the time to tell you.

Most states will pay for up to five years tuition for you to attend college, if you are going to be on the program take advantage of all it has to offer, The Clinton Administration placed a five-year time limit on benefits. In five years, you could have at least got a bachelor's degree at best. Your childcare is taken care of, your medical benefits, are 100 percent paid for because no one is telling you about all these benefits, this is no reason to remain on assistance for years and years. You must ask questions and do your research. I am fully aware of all of the disadvantages, but I want to focus on telling you what to do so you can get off and stay off. Most states will allow you to save up to $5000.00 in assets, they have a program that will assist you in purchasing a car.

If you have a job, that is more than a fifty-mile radius and it is hindering you from getting to work, they will either, help you get a free car or a refurbished car. The Housing Authority has a program that will assist you in cleaning up your credit and helping you not only to purchase a HUD house but will assist you with up to 30 percent of the mortgage for the first five or ten years, a separate bank account will be setup to go toward your down payment. They will also connect you with organizations in the community who will match dollar for dollar, to help with your down payment. They will also give you a voucher, for brand new furniture for your new home, these programs vary from state to state, But the good news is if you live in a state and they don't have these programs, if you have a Section 8 voucher, you can port out to any of the 50 states in America. If you live in California and the cost of living is too high and they don't offer a particular program in that State, you can move to a State where the cost of living is low, citing financial hardship because of the high cost to live. I was hired by the State because I was on assistance at the time, if you have a good work history your chances of being hired by the state is very good. I would bounce back and forth between Philadelphia and Maryland when I went through my divorce (Different Book, lol) I moved in with my mother who was living in public housing, because I was her daughter, although I was grown with kids, I applied with the Philadelphia Housing Authority and because of this program I was hired, I stayed there for ten years. I want to express to you that you do not have to stay stuck, there is always a way out. I learned so much being on both sides, working in the programs and being on the programs when I needed to apply, I did because my tax dollars were going in that bucket as well. I want you to take advantage of everything these programs have to offer, use this as a stepping stone to a better life, break the cycle of **POVERTY** off your life, it is just a word, it only has the power that you give it. You are wealthy, and you have greatness locked on the inside of you. My job is to make you aware, wake you up to the possibilities because at any moment they can pull the rug from up under you and close those programs down. If they see you are trying to help yourself, so many doors of opportunities will open for you. The clients on my caseload I made sure they knew about every program that was available to them, I took a lot of flak because my fellow co-workers, who were all a paycheck away from collecting food stamps themselves, would only do the bare minimum. The cost of living in Annapolis is very high, so they are barely making it, while withholding information that could benefit the clients.

These are just a few of the benefits that you can take advantage of to use this as a stepping stone to be on your own. One last lesson, some states will allow you to have your own business, the programs are income-based, so that means you can still make money, up to a certain amount. I will cover these discrepancies, and disadvantages in the next chapter. Know this, you are not lazy, your ancestors built a whole civilization without modern day tools, greatness is in your DNA, do not allow the rules and guidelines that are negative to define you, you can **ERASE, ERADICATE & ANNIHILATE POVERTY** from your life. I did it you can too, I have been where you are, walked in your shoes, felt how you feel, but I knew how to get out and how to use it to my advantage. I wrote this book with you in mind, do not allow yourself to be engulfed in that negative environment, break away from the pack. I know they will talk about you, so what. I know how it is when they see you going to college to better yourself, they will tell you all kinds of things, don't listen to that mess, Listen to me, I know the rules, I have been on both sides, do not listen when they say, who she thinks she is, don't respond, show them who you are, because guess what, it's going to help them in the long run. God created everything to be free, get out of the container of **POVERTY**; it is a Goliath that can be defeated. Call your case manager and ask her some questions, go on the HUD website and find out what houses they have for sale before Ben Carson eliminates the program all together. Make a decision right now, set financial goals for yourself, tell yourself, I am giving myself one more year to get off and stand on my own, at the end of this book I will give you an opportunity to do what I call a PTC with me, it is my gift to you for purchasing this book, Personal Touch Coaching™ where you can contact me, and I will answer your questions and help to guide you in the right direction. When you do your part, God is faithful to do His part.

THE END OF POVERTY, HOW CAN WE MAKE IT HAPPEN IN YOUR LIFETIME?

Dear Mr. President

This book was written to address the needs and concerns of the American citizens; I wanted to use this book as a catalyst to enact real change. Because I have worked for the government on all three levels, it has afforded me a very unique perspective. I want to address those in the chapter, although the programs created for those who find themselves facing financial challenges, one thing is clear, those programs also have a duality. The same programs that were created to help, are also hurting people and causing them to be trapped, for not only years but generations of families find themselves caught up in the bureaucracy which is the Federal government, with its complexity of policies that are obsolete and outdated. I am not one to complain but I am one to act, a world changer, so I decided to write a letter to the President of this United States of America and politely inform him of the disadvantages that these programs possess and how they are crippling our people.

Millions of Americans find themselves struggling to make ends meet. Despite improvements in the job market and a housing bounce back, there are still many people who need help to stay afloat financially. In many ways, the America of today mirrors that of the Depression-era, when the first national welfare system was introduced.

Welfare programs were originally designed to help stabilize the economy and get struggling families back on their feet, a goal that's often overshadowed by the stereotypes and misconceptions people tend to have about the system in general.

More facts: Children are more likely to be on welfare than adults with 38% of kids aged 5 and under living in households that receive public assistance. Almost 35% of kids aged 6 to 10 and 32% of those in the 11-to15-year-old range are on welfare.

Here's the breakdown of welfare recipients: 16.3% of Non-Hispanic Whites. 39.7% of Non-Hispanic Blacks. 36.4% of Hispanics. Hispanics represent the fastest rate of growth for any demographic group (a 15% increase since the year 2000). These numbers are constantly changing, so as you can see the system needs to be fixed. There are dozens of state and federally sponsored welfare programs. When you consider them all collectively, it comes to around $1 trillion in spending each year. This is the purpose for this chapter, to create a win-win situation, where the American citizens can get off and out of the system, and also save the government, millions of dollars, money that can be allocated to helping those in need like our veterans, and senior citizens who have made significant contributions to society and deserve to be treated better.

I know that I am the perfect person to address this issue because I have been on both sides and I know what needs to be changed and more importantly, I know how to change it. The people that normally write these policies have never struggled, if you are going to create a program to help me at least understand my struggle. The people receiving these benefits are not just Black people, so let's dispel that myth, we are facing a crisis of epic proportion, we are spending trillions of dollars on a system that are not working, let's fix it. These programs are only supplements, families that receive food stamps are still going to bed hungry, they are not designed to last the entire month. Supplement means in addition too, most of these people do not work, because, for every dollar they make, a dollar is taken away from them, so it becomes more feasible for them to stay on assistance. The cash assistance is very little, I remember growing up my mother she could not buy us clothes to wear to school, I could not participate in school activities, I was on the track team, when it came time to pay for uniforms I had to quit, my mother did not have the money. I joined the school choir, headed by Mr. Gabriel Hardeman, it was an honor to be chosen to sing on his choir, I had to leave the choir, my mother did not have money to buy my robe or money for me to travel with the choir. I could not take pictures on picture day when the school went on field trips, I was the child who was sent to another classroom because my class went on the trip, I did not have the money to go. I know these things are not important to you and they are not your responsibility, but there are some very fundamental things that are being left out and overlooked. If helping someone is hurting them in the long run, is it really help?

I want you to look past the surface, past the stereotypes, past the color of their skin and into the humanity of a people you are called to and vowed to serve. I want you to look at it, as if it were you, or your mother or someone that you know, What changes would you make, to benefit them, not only in the interim but long-term, so that America can utilize the treasure buried deep inside the hearts of a people in distress, disappointed, discouraged, and that feel forgotten and lost. I want to stir up your compassion, empathy, sympathy as you read this book. I want you to think about the plethora of situations that can happen in a persons' life that will cause them to apply for these programs temporarily and end up stuck because the policy writer's vision was skewed and tainted, not by facts, but rumors of people buying junk food, or selling food stamps, or eating filet mignon with their tax dollars, we don't need a hand out, just a hand up. You never know when life will happen to you, you never know what situation you will find yourself in, life happens to us all. Stop placing people in boxes according to the zeros in their bank account. I know the value of money, I studied finance in college, I teach money, but I teach money in its proper place. Money is not a tool that should be used to separate people into classes. Lower class, Middle Class, Upper Class, this type of division is crippling, not only to our people but our country. I was taught all of the social graces by my grandmother, she was determined that living in the container I call **POVERTY** was not going to define me. She taught me not only how to cook a three-course, five-course, and seven- course meals, but the Joy of Cooking was as taple in her kitchen. I was taught how to use the proper fork, how to set a table and eat a seven-course meal, she wanted me to be able to conversate with the President or talk Ebonics with my friends. The holidays were a special time, we ate on linen table clothes and the finest china her money could buy. What does how much money you have or not have to do with how I live? I determine the quality of my life and character, money cannot buy class. Do not look down on people because your parents had money and mine did not, because money can't buy character, you can be a billionaire and still be a baphoon, rich in dollars and broke in character. I was not taught the so-called white way, I was taught the right way, to do things correctly, is the definition of etiquette. She did not want me to fit into the box the government created for me, I was not only black, I was human.

Create programs based on humanity, not color, as the stats show there are more Non-whites receiving assistance. I implore you today, take a look from inside the heart of someone who has been there, from someone who cares not just about my people, but all people. Money does not dictate the quality of life, I remember transitioning from one state to another, I was starting over yet again, I had very little money, but I was traveling, eating at five-star restaurants , visiting wonderful places, I always had nice clothes, meeting wonderful people, it was at this time that I realized money has nothing to do with the quality of my life, it is not where you live, but how you live, as my grandmother used to say, you don't live outside, make your home into a palace. If you have never been low on a dime, how can you write a policy for those who have? So, since I have the inside scoop, I figured I would help you out.

Dear Mr. /Mrs. President

I hope this letter finds you in good spirits. I am a public servant, who had the pleasure of working for the State of Maryland, Department of Social Services. I am writing this letter out of care and concern for those participating in the program, in an effort to make it more beneficial for both parties. I am well versed in the policy regarding (SNAP)

Supplemental Nutrition Program, (TCA) Temporary Cash Assistance and (MA) Medical Assistance. In the time that I worked for the Department of Social Services, this experience has afforded me the opportunity to see the programs advantages and disadvantages. I would like to inform you of the discrepancies or ways the programs can be improved to help not only the recipients but to save the Federal government millions of dollars that can be allocated to other programs that we need, like our Veterans, or Senior Citizens.

I have enclosed a proposal of potential policy changes that you will find beneficial to the citizens of this great United States of America.

I thank you for your time, I look forward to your prompt response.

Sincerely

Sharon D. "Skyy" Chase

Sharon D, "Skyy" Chase

I decided to write this letter so that laws, ordinances; policies can be changed for the greater good of humankind. I wrote this letter for every single mother struggling to make ends meet, for every veteran who has fought for our earthly freedom and came home to struggle financially, with food and housing because of the effects of war, I wrote this for the senior citizens who are now retired and have to choose between buying food or medicine and lastly, for the millions of children that go to bed hungry every night because they are trapped in the container I call **POVERTY**, and for those that I may have missed, the journey that I have walked and all that I have been through, this is for you. There are many people who I meet and pray for daily. Who would rather live on the street, than to be trapped in these programs. That is very telling, these programs are a form of oppression, it's time to let these people go.

I decided to Google – Dear Mr. President, it is a habit I have because I create programs, so I always go to the Go Daddy to see if the name I created is taken and I stumbled upon something so wonderful. The artist PINK, who I love her music wrote a song called guess what, – "Dear Mr. President, I did not know it in all honesty, Ecc. 3. A time for every purpose, it's time. I will share the lyrics it is so appropriate for this chapter

Dear Mr. President,

Come take a walk with me

Let's pretend we're just two people and

You're not better than me

I'd like to ask you some questions if we can speak honestly

What do you feel when you see all the homeless on the street?

Who do you pray for at night before you go to sleep?

What do you feel when you look in the mirror?

Are you proud?

How do you sleep while the rest of us cry?

How do you dream when a mother has no chance to say?

goodbye?

How do you walk with your head held high?

Can you even look me in the eye?

And tell me why?

Dear Mr. President

Were you a lonely boy?

Are you a lonely boy?

Are you a lonely boy?

How can you say, no

child is left behind?

We're not dumb, and we're not blind

They're all sitting in your cells

While you pave the road to hell

What kind of father would take his own daughter's rights away?

And what kind of father might hate his own daughter if she were lesbian?

I can only imagine what the first lady has to say

You've come a long way from whiskey and cocaine

How do you sleep while the rest of us cry?

How do you dream when a mother has no chance
to say goodbye?

ow do you walk with your head held high?

Can you even look me in the eye?

Let me tell you 'bout hard work

Minimum wage with a baby on the way

Let me tell you 'bout hard work

Rebuilding your house after the bombs took them away

Let me tell you 'bout hard work

Building a bed out of a cardboard box

Let me tell you 'bout hard work

Hard work

Hard work

You don't know nothing 'bout hard work

Hard work

Hard work

Oh!

How do you sleep at night?

How do you walk with your head held
high?

Dear Mr. President

You'd never take a walk with me

Would you?

Songwriters: Alicia Moore, William Mann

© Sony/ATV Music Publishing LLC, BMG Rights Management

Wow, I could not believe it, I knew this was no coincidence and that I was supposed to write this book at this time. The mantra of my life to everything there is a season and a time to every purpose under the heaven… It is time, time for a change in this country.

Proposal for Change

I learned to create programs at my church and on my job, like I told you, I was always the person everyone came to for answers, I am an Administrator by functionality, highly organized and can multi-task efficiently, doing many things at one time. I am the person who has a thousand tabs open on her computer as well as in her brain. Creating programs, negotiating contracts, time management, are all things I learned working as a public servant in different parts of the government, all transferable skills, we will talk about that later, in this chapter, I want to look at the disadvantages of these programs and how we can fix them. I am a change agent, which means I take action. People tend to complain about problems, but never seek out the solutions. I will only submit a snapshot of the proposed changes that I will be submitting to the Federal government, in the form of the Executive Summary, but allow me to address the word change, we fight against the thing that we need to help us because it comes in the form of change. You might be afraid of change because it will affect the way others see you. Don't be afraid of what people think! Let go of the pride that you may have and be willing to make a leap of faith. Don't worry about failing, everyone messes up sometimes. Allow yourself some grace and prepare yourself for the possibility of success. This will only make you a stronger person! Just be sure to learn from your mistakes. Ask yourself this question: "Am I learning?" If the answer is "yes", you're on the right track.

Change is never easy, but it is always a good thing. If you have experienced change, embrace it and make it work for you. If you want to change something in your life, start by making small changes and don't be afraid, fear is an illusion. Success and growth are just around the corner when you stop rejecting change and start accepting it instead. I propose these changes to start, this will be written and submitted in a formal, government document, this is real, I don't chase money, I chase purpose. I am still advocating, fighting and slaying giants. Do you think I worked at every government level for nothing, I am putting everything I learned on assignment to use because I'm called to a nation, that nation is You.

Executive Summary: In the proposal, I will submit changes to the SNAP program by suggesting that all states enact a uniform policy concerning Welfare to Work Initiative

1. Adopt a uniform policy by all 50 states giving recipients, at a minimum of six months of transitional food stamps, giving them the time necessary time to save money and remain off assistance,
2. Adopt a uniform policy by all 50 states making it mandatory for recipients to receive nutrition classes, budgeting, financial management, and life skills necessary to exit the assistance roles permanently.
3. Adopt a uniform policy by all 50 states giving recipients six months or longer cash assistance while in the Welfare to

Work program to cover incidentals such as transportation, clothing allowances, etc.
4. Adopt a uniform policy by all 50 stated, to utilize the human resources for recipients who have prior work experience, partner with Federal, City, State government agencies to fill vacant spots and give those who qualify a job.
5. Adopt a uniform policy by all 50 states to all allow recipients, to have assets up to $10,000, to be earmarked for the purchase of housing, starting a business, to ensure the permanent exiting off the roles and saving the Federal government millions of dollars.

The program is set up to incentivize the recipient to remain on assistance, we must create incentives for them to get off of assistance, these are just a few of the proposals that I will be submitting to the United States Department of Agriculture, they regulate these programs, but they are carried out on the state level. These changes must be carried out uniformly and not based on budget items determined by individual agencies. For example, let's look at Maryland, when you become gainfully employed you will receive what is called transitional food stamps, meaning they will not take money from you dollar for dollar because you are working, But this is great, but what is missing is most people do not budget, and that goes for people who are not on assistance, I worked as personal advisor for Wells Fargo, people with money, do not budget. People are under the misconception that budgeting is for people with money. That is a fallacy, a budget serves as a way to track money, the amount is not important. In Texas, they do not give transitional food stamps to recipients who find employment, meaning once they start working, according to how much they receive, the food stamp amount will be greatly reduced, so people feel like it is better to stay on assistance than to find a job. The program must be comprehensive, and some aspects must be made mandatory so that participation will not be a factor.

I shared with you how I was hired at the Department of Social Services, I was a recipient and my unemployment had run out, I do not believe that I worked there just so that I can benefit. I want to take what I have learned and help you to successfully exit the roles and build the life you imagined for yourself because these programs will not be around for long, they are already trying to find ways to do away with them. Our current President is proposing to sending people food boxes, it is time to get off, on your own and not wait for them to further degrade and marginalize you because of the status of your bank account. I am here to remind you that you are a Diamond, oh no this not fluff, I am not gassing you up. I am completely serious, you have everything it takes to build the life you want for yourself. It's like wanting a cake and looking at every else's cake, when all you need to do put your ingredients together from your kitchen and make your own cake, I am here to tell you to make your own cake, make your own money, do not chase after money, you have the capacity and the capability to make your own money. Once you tap into your talent, money becomes very easy to make. Money is a by-product of talent, grit, determination, and perseverance, just because you started out on assistance, you do not have to stay there. If you find yourself there for whatever reason, use it to your advantage, find out all the program has to offer, and use it as a stepping stone to a better life. One thing I saw growing up is none of the adults worked, they all collected assistance, and if someone did decide to work, they ridiculed them. That must stop, the women only stuck together because when one ran out of food they would go to the food pantry and stand in line for that hard government cheese that blocked you up for the rest of the year. It did make good grill cheese sandwiches, though I can't front but seriously, I hated standing in lines for handouts, to this day to me **POVERTY** reminds me of standing in a line waiting for someone to give me something. You have the butter, eggs, water, flour, sugar to make your own cake. You are smart, brilliant, intelligent, strong, talented and gifted beyond measure, if you have the survival skills to make in the jungle of low – income every day, you have what it takes to make money, your talent lying dormant on the inside of you is the potential to make a million dollars at a minimum. You are walking around allowing a government program designed to keep you stuck to determine your destiny, when you have money sitting in you in the form of ideas, and inventions. Instead of watching Love &Hip Hop, Atlanta Housewives, you are helping the ratings by watching them, they are making money and you are wasting time watching. Kandi Burrus is my Shero, she is the most enterprising person I know, I had the pleasure of meeting her and will work with her in the near future, but I can't sit back and watch her make money, I can't spend her money. Make your own money, it is easier than you think especially with Social Media. The adults did not work, I never heard anyone talk about their dreams or goals, I just watched them waste time doing nothing every day. I shared with you my love for reading, my first job was at the Central Library downtown branch in Philadelphia, I was resourceful, my paycheck was sponsored by the Catholic Archdiocese. I am not a Catholic, but if they were willing to pay my salary, then I was willing to work, I was a clerical aide, my first supervisor name was Jean Melbourne. I loved working downtown at the beautiful library, across the street was Logan Circle, a water fountain, with beautiful sculpture spewed out water on a hot summer day, I would sit there and eat my lunch, it added color to my world. I fought a poverty mindset daily, how did I make it out, by keeping my righteous mind, you can too, do not settle for less than the best that life has to offer, no one will give it to you. You must fight for it, you deserve it, you are worth it. Do not allow anyone to judge you based on a temporary situation or circumstance, life happens to the best of us. Be determined, tell yourself, I am coming out of this; decision is the open door to reality.

These experiences all helped to shape my life, the good, the bad and the ugly, When I started my consulting business, God told me to gather my pearls, I took the best of my gifts, abilities, talents, education/experiences and skills and poured them into my business. I educate, empower, inspire, motivate, teach Money & Business to emerging entrepreneurs. God uses everything, he wastes nothing. My business is thriving because working at all these different places, I became an Administrator, but of my own resources. I learned diversity from dealing with people from all walks of life and socio-economic backgrounds. I am building my empire and finally living my dreams. I walked this journey to share with you, if I can do it, you can too. When you change your mind, it will change the trajectory of your life. It is never too late, but the time is Now!

Section III Productive Solutions

Change your mind—It's your Perogative

In these next chapters, I am going to share with some of the classes, workshops, seminars, and programs that I have created over the years. I started creating programs for my church, my job and never ever knew that I could sell these programs and make money. I eventually got tired of working for other people, it was time for me to use my talents to help myself. I had gone through my life helping everyone else, but my dreams were dying on the back burner of my life, I had gotten married at the age of 19, and had children, and living my dreams where the furthest thing from my mind. I focused on being a wife and mother and this took up the majority of my life. I changed my mind and decided I was going to resurrect my dreams, but I did not know what I was going to do because I had a wealth of experience, a wealth of talent, a wealth of knowledge, I told you I decided while sitting on my favorite statue in Fairmount Park that I was Wealthy. It is the most frustrating thing to know that you have wealth on the inside, but how do I manifest it. I loved to write down my thoughts in my journal, so I wrote it down in a business plan and began to manifest my dreams.

Everything you see began as a thought in someone's mind. The chair you sit on. The table you work at. The car you drive. The house you live in. The clothes you wear. The television you watch.

First a thought. Then, a thing brought from nothing. Everything begins as a thought. The verb for turning thoughts into things is to manifest. It comes from the Middle English word "manifesto" meaning invisible and the Latin word meaning "hand". Put your hands to work so God can prosper them.

When you manifest something, you reach your hand through the invisible curtain separating the tangible world from the world of imagination and pull your desired object into existence. First, you think it, then you manifest it. You materialize it. You cause it to appear. Everyone manifest. Some people manifest abundance. Others manifest lack. What am I saying, (I am not (New Age) If you don't have what you want, examine your thoughts. Change your mind, wealthy people are wealthy because they think different.

Rich people believe money is earned through thinking, while the average person believes money is earned through time and labor.

The middle class thinks about money in linear terms, Siebold explains, *"they believe the only way to earn more money is to work more hours."*

"The wealthy know big money requires thinking about it in non- linear terms," he writes. "*The rich know that creative thinking is the highest paid skill in the world…Training* your mind to find solutions to difficult problems are the real secret to making money." What did I say, all my life people came to me for answers, how do you make money by solving problems? That is how you manifest. This is how Chase Wealth Solutions was born; I created a business that provides answers, to the masses, Take Action, Do It, If You can dream it, you can achieve it, sounds cliché, but so true.

One thing I became good at is being resourceful, and creative, neither one cost a dime. You think your problem is lack of money, your problem is not lack of money, it is the lack of the ability to think your way out of a situation. Wealthy people are thinkers that are why they read books, to feed their mind information to help them solve problems. How do you make money by solving problems, not just for yourself but for other people? Money is a measure of value, it is how we measure services and goods, not people, you are priceless, someone died for you and deemed you priceless, you can't put my self-worth on a spreadsheet, but I can place a value on my services and goods, that I exchange in the marketplace for money. The price of products rises the more scarcity or in demand the product, you are a Diamond, a diamond is the most sought-after gemstone, why because of perceived value, and the scarcity, but mainly because of its unique qualities. Remember, the diamond when mined, it is kept in its natural form, with inclusions, blemishes, it is given a grade, but it still carries intrinsic value. The time it takes to mine the diamond, take it through the process of pressure, and other various stages, it is priced and placed on the market in exchange for MONEY. So, what should you be mining for in your life, you should be mining for your talent that is hidden deep inside you, your million-dollar idea that you had, a year went by and you saw someone else capitalizing on it on QVC or HSN.

The first process I talked about was clarity, your mind must stay clear from all the distractions around you, you must protect your mind and renew it daily. One of the reasons I love reading books is because it is the quickest way to see a new perspective, you are reading from someone else's point for view, this causes your mind to open up to different possibilities. You may not have the money to travel at this moment, but you can travel in a book, and add color to your world. If you are around the same people, saying the same negative things every day gossiping, all day, how do you think your mind will be affected? Every day I would leave out of the projects, go to museums, sit in the park, visit my grand mom, go to the Chamber, find out what was going on in Philadelphia, I joined all kinds of programs. You would have never known I was financially challenged, I never accepted it because I decided I was wealthy, so I acted like it, not in an arrogant or prideful way. When Oprah came on I would always say, she is living my life. I will live that life, go to college, get a PhD, not an honorary, but one that I earned; you can't put Dr. in front of your name if someone gives you a degree that you do not matriculate for, that was my goal. I am coming for you Oprah. (LOL) I know I should have gone to college for journalism; I am always walking up to complete strangers with my invisible microphone to interview them and ask them a thousand questions. I love it, they always answer me. I need to get my Master's - Journalism, get some real news, get rid of the fake news. Don't get me started (I digressed).

Change your mind, I have watched people allow their minds to be taken as a result of their situation, I watched the darkness that was supposed to make them crush them under the weight of the pressure. I watched them succumbed to drugs, alcohol, prostitution looking for the way out, not realizing that the way out was inside of them. I had friends as young as eight- and nine-years-old smoke, weed, cigarettes, sell drugs because this was all that is emulated in front of them. All of my friends smoked cigarettes and weed at an early age, I did not indulge in that until I was fifteen and that is still too young. To this day, I don't smoke, drink or do drugs, its altars your mind, hearing about people overdosing on drugs is a normal everyday occurrence. You do not have to allow the pressure of your environment to crush you, protect your mind at all cost. It is your mind that you use to make you the money that you desire.

I started a book club in 2013, exclusively for young men and adult men called **Company of Men Book Review Club**, the reason it is exclusive to men is because, I want to dispel the myth that men don't read, especially Black men. I was watching a documentary about schools, I was astonished to find out that the prison system based the number of prisons it builds on the number of African American students that drop out of ninth grade, The Prison Industrial Complex is a billion-dollar industry. People a library card is free. I want you to know that black men do read, and it does not make you a sissy or girly if you do read. Change your mind, reading and studying is the quickest way to receive an impartation and upgrade old information. Renew your mind daily, don't just read your Bible, study it, commit it to memory,

I will leave the website and the end of the book for those who are interested can join. Remember the commercial; the mind is a terrible thing to waste". When you change your mind, you can manifest your money. Which leads me to the next topic, Money.

Make Friends with Money- Not Chase It or Love It

This chapter is critical if you are going to be free of poverty, it starts with your mindset. We formulate the narratives in our lives based on experiences. A mindset means you have one way of thinking about a subject matter. Your mindset is shaped by trauma, hurts or lies that you have been told; making friends with money allows you to examine your beliefs about money and change the narrative. I call it rewriting your wealth story. In order to achieve it, you must ask yourself some hard questions and then change the answers accordingly.

What is your relationship with money?

How do I feel about money?

What are my beliefs about money?

We operate from experiences and messages given to us from our past and what we learn along the way. These influences can hinder how we deal with money.

In other words; your relationship with money has to do with behavior and patterns in your feelings and emotions. Have you ever heard of Curtis "Wall Street" Carroll, this young man is incarcerated, a convicted murderer, overcame poverty, taught himself to be financially?

literate, he is currently serving a life term? He created a program called "FEEL" Financial Empowerment Emotional Literacy, he teaches the importance of separating your emotions from your money decisions. The definition of poor is not lack of money, its greed, and selfishness. You can be a giver and still be selfish.

How you feel about money reflects the deepest fears to the most heartfelt desires on a daily basis.

Money - Emotional Connection

Why do some people idolize money?

Money is their God. Making friends with money is not the same as worshipping money.

Why are some people afraid of money or they believe that wanting money is unworthy or even a shameful goal?

Why do some people kill for money or kill themselves if they lose it all?

Why do close relatives, spouses, or friends become enemies over money?

The answers lie in your belief system and how you have been taught about money. Maybe your parents were stingy with you or poor to a fault. When your life is tough, and money was limited, and you were told to feel grateful for the money you get. Or in contrast, you were raised to be greedy with money. Whatever you were taught or believe, there is always an emotional component to money.

When you think about money, do you feel sad, depressed, worthy, unworthy, deserving, guilty, secure, happy, entitled, fearful?

Your attitudes about money can affect and drive your financial goals.

If you feel deep down inside that your fate is to struggle and never have enough, then you have a poverty mentality.

MONEY CATEGORIES

The MONEY Chasers – they measure how much money they have as success. They brag about how much money they make. They have energy and drive to make things happen. Weaknesses are financial management, they spend money on non-essentials. I.e., instead of cooking balanced home cooked meals, they eat out every day. Because they can afford luxury items they tend to want to keep up with the Joneses, they are very competitive. Do you see the correlation between money and emotion or behavior? Money chasers are so busy equating money with success, they tend to have a superior and condescending attitude toward other people, but it is disguised as humility. They equate money with self-worth, this is what drives them, Money is a pacifier to them, it makes them feel secure. If you examine their lives closely, they started chasing money at a young age, it is their way of being accepted. They will be the main ones to argue you down, that money is not their God.

Money Belief Systems

Money equals Power – Money rules them. The richer I am, the more I can call the shots, they want to be in control. Money rules them, if I have a lot of money, I will be free, and then I could use the money to sponsor a meaningful cause. They feel in control but in reality, money is controlling them. Maslow's Hierarchy of Needs… They are driven and motivated by money. Money is their dominant thought, that's all they talk about and that's all they think about. In today's society, if you have the gift of gab, a charismatic personality, throw in some consistency and you know marketing, you can make tons of money. Examine your motives, it is important to put money in its proper perspective.

Money equals Self-Worth– they measure there worth as a person by how much money they have or invested or saved. They feel that without money they are no one, they bank their self-worth on what they have in the bank. Your self-worth and your net-worth are two separate things. Self-worth can't be measured on a spreadsheet.

Money equals Security – there inner peace is dependent on financial security.

Money equals Love – they believe if I have money people will love me. They buy the love of friends, loved ones by giving gifts, but nothing can take the place nurturing affection, or attention. They take care of everyone else when in reality, it is showboating.

Money equals opiate – If you feel sad, lonely, angry, abandoned, empty, then you are using money as a medicine. You are filling the void with money. They believe money can ease emotional pain, smooth the difficult times in life, buy pleasure. You must separate emotion from money because money magnifies.

Money Equals Prestige– They believe money can bring them respect and admiration of others.

Money equals Happiness – If they have money they will be happy. Money can provide pleasure. Happiness is a state of mind.

It's important to have a healthy relationship with money…don't chase money, don't love money, just make money your friend. You will have a friend for life.

How do you make friends with money?

Money is a tool to be used for something, to do something, to accomplish a purpose.

Find out what the purpose for money is in your life, not to brag about how much you have.

Put money in the proper perspective in your life; build a life based on quality, morality, integrity without money. Do you know who you are without money or have you been dreaming of being a millionaire since high school. There is nothing wrong with having a big bank account, the love of money is the root of all evil. It is a slippery slope, be forewarned.

Give your money a mission, then your money will work for you, instead of you working for your money, this is the difference between being rich or poor. I put this chapter in the book because I want you to stop chasing money and examine your relationship with money. It is key to making money, I remember when I was thirteen, I asked my stepfather for a bicycle, I was tired of walking or taking the bus. My birthday was coming, and I never asked for anything, my stepdad always had a job. He asked me what I wanted for my birthday, I told him I wanted a bicycle. My birthday came around and he did not buy me the bike like he promised, he gave me a $50.00-dollarbill. I was so hurt and angry I tore the $50.00 up and flushed it down the toilet, my mother almost had a heart attack. I would later learn that this affected my relationship with money; I had always felt like you can't buy me, sway me or move me with your money. I watched women sell their bodies, people sell drugs, they do anything for money. I saw money have control over people's lives, they allowed something that was created to give things value, devalue them. I had money in the right perspective, but it was one thing missing, I did not respect money; I had to learn to respect money because if you treated it like a person it would come to you easily and effortlessly. Once I examined my relationship with money, it allowed me to teach other people to do the same, then money came to me effortlessly.

You would be surprised at how you treat money, do you spend every dime you get, are you stingy, do you share, are you greedy with your money? Poverty is not the lack of money, a poverty mentality is people who are selfish and greedy with their money, they are never satisfied no matter how much they make. They are greedy and fearful of ending up with no money back where they started. This is the reason someone can win millions of dollars in the lottery and end up with no money in a short amount of time. The relationship with money, they have not examined it, this is a key to building wealth.

Money is the result of time, labor, talent, the end product. Why is Oprah a billionaire, because she has exchanged her talent for money? What is the difference between you and Oprah, Tyler Perry, Warren Buffet, Beyoncé, Tiger Woods and a host of other people. These people are no better, they realized that they have plenty of money on the inside of them in the form of talent. I want you to make friends with money, so that you can keep it in perspective and not make money your God. You have the ability to make plenty of money, but once you make it, I want you to know how to keep it. You may not exhibit all of these characteristics, but the ones you do, make a change. You have the power, it has been given to you, to obtain your wealth, you don't need government assistance, you need this book, to open your eyes to the possibilities that are unlimited within you.

Talent is synonymous with money, I have been gifted with the ability to recognize people's talents. My children growing up knew what heir talents, gifts, and callings were. I would pray for them and God would reveal them to me. I noticed over the years as I studied talent, that it brings order to your life. In my business, I help people discover their talent, your talent is your ATM. In order for you to make money, you must exchange, your talent, time, skills in the marketplace for money. The other person is not better than you, they have discovered what makes them money, so many people's talent stays buried in the dark place, hidden from them and never shared with the world. God has given each person at least one talent, and that one talent has the potential at a minimum to make you a millionaire. Remember, the analogy of the Diamond, every diamond has value, every person has value, buried deep within, it is the pressure, process and time that reveals the true value. I have created several programs in my business where I work with my clients to discover the treasure within because it is my job to walk alongside of you on this journey. There is a special place in my heart for the underdog because I want to see you win.

In these next chapters, I will share with you what I have to offer to help you not only get out of your present situation but to stay out. These programs are designed to help you turn your financial situation around and live to your fullest potential.

In closing, money is a result of doing something, it is a byproduct. Money is a way to measure, time, labor and talent. No one can put a price on you, but they can place a price on a thing. You are not a thing, do not allow people to tell you that you are less than because of the number of zeros and commas in your bank account. You have talent which can be exchanged in the marketplace for money. You must be intentional about becoming financially independent. You must start by investing in yourself, read a book, hire a coach, make an intelligent, informed decision. If you didn't know before, now you do, by discovering your talent you unlock your wealth, Cha Ching now your bank account will grow,

Let's start by changing the way we think, you can't put new wine into old wine skins, Affirmations are critical, say them to yourself for the next 30 days, I challenge you to say them daily, out with the old and in with the new.

It has been my pleasure to share my stories with you I pray that they are life-changing and inspiring. My prayer is that you take heed to the words that I have written, they are heartfelt. I am concerned about each and every one of you, you can overcome and win against the Spirit of Poverty. You are in my prayers, God has not forgotten about you. God Bless

The next chapters I will give you some resources to help you daily.

Affirmations

Affirmations are important when cancelling out all the negative words you hear, or that you speak. In order to cancel out negative talk, it takes seven times to say an affirming word. You must guard your heart and mind at all times. It is time to change the mindset and write a new narrative for your life.

I pray for wisdom for finances.
Blessed be the Lord, who daily loads us with benefits, even the God of our salvation.
Psalms 68:19

God wishes above all things that we would prosper and be in health, even as our soul prospers. With God's help…I am prospering. I am in health. My soul is prospering.
3 John 1:2

The whole earth is the Lord's.
All that I am and all that I have belongs to the Lord. My goal is to always be a good steward over all God has trusted me with.
Psalms 24:1

The Lord multiplies all of my resources.
I am increasing. God's blessings are always more than enough.
Psalms 115:14

As the Word says – God opens His hand and satisfies the desire of every living thing.
God is bigger than any financial challenge I will ever face.
Psalms 145:16

The Lord has given us the power to get wealth, so that we may help to establish His covenant and spread the gospel. I take action daily to improve my finances. God's economy is always a great economy and filled with Blessings!
Deuteronomy 8:18

I pray that everything that God has called me to do will continue to prosper.
I am blessed going in and blessed going
out. I am blessed to be a blessing to others.
Deuteronomy 28:6

The blessing of the Lord, it makes us rich, and He adds no sorrow with it.
I am being led to true prosperity – including things money cannot buy.
Proverbs 10:22

With God's blessings… we attract riches, and honor, and the abundant life.
Proverbs 22:4

In everything, I give thanks to the Lord!
I keep the words of God's covenant, and do them, that I may prosper in all that I do.
I am thankful for all of my blessings.
Deuteronomy 29:9

30 Day Affirmation Challenge

There are endless opportunities to excel surrounding me

I have the vision to see opportunities in every situation and make the best use of them

I boldly and promptly act on opportunities when I see them. I have a strong intuition to lead me to the opportunities. I discover my hidden potential with every opportunity. With my unique skills and talents, I am making a profound positive difference in the world

I am meant to do great things in life

I always follow my heart and discover my destiny

I am making this world better and beautiful with my unique contribution

My life is filled with great abundance in all areas

There are abundance and prosperity all around me.

I am grateful to the universe for fulfilling my every desire

As my commitment to help others grows, so does my wealth. I receive continuous opportunities to increase my wealth. Money comes to me easily and effortlessly

My wealth keeps on increasing with every passing day. I am enjoying my financial independence

I easily see the lesson or the blessing in all that is.

A river of compassion washes away my anger and replaces it with love.

I am peaceful in my body, heart, and soul.

I am superior to negative thoughts and low actions.

All is well in my world. Everything is working out for my highest good. Out of this situation, only good will come. I am safe!

I forgive those who have harmed me in my past and peacefully detach from them.

My body is healthy; my mind is brilliant; my soul is tranquil. I am healthy, whole, and complete.

As I say yes to life, life says yes to me.

I possess the qualities needed to be extremely successful.

Everything that is happening now is happening for the ultimate good.

Creative energy surges through me and leads me to new and brilliant ideas.

Today, I abandon my old habits and take up new, more positive ones.

The point of power is always in the present moment. I press on because I believe in my path.

I am courageous, and I stand up for myself.

My thoughts are filled with prosperity.

Happiness is a choice. I base my happiness on my own accomplishments and the blessings I've been given

Many people look up to me and recognize my worth; I am admired. Every thought we think is creating our future.

B.Y.O B – BE YOUR OWN BOSS
Startup Niches
Creative Ideas

Arts & crafts
Business Consultant
Interior Designer
Jewelry

Doing What You Love

Freelancing your expertise
Hobby business
Sports business
Product Sales
Direct sales
eBay
Gift basket

B-to-B Businesses

Bookkeeping
Business support

Consulting/Coaching
Web Design
Invoicing
Medical claims
Payments
Security specialist
Seminar production
Transcription service
Virtual assistant business

Most Popular Online Payment Solutions

Personal Services
Child-care
Elder Care
Financial Advisor
Organizer
Personal
Concierge
Personal Shopper
Tutoring service
Wedding consultant
Cleaning
Event planning
Mobile photography
Taxes
Social Media Agency

Trademark™- Signature Programs

These are a few of the newest programs I created to help you achieve your financial goals. These programs have all been trademarked and copywritten, they are for exclusive use of the owner and cannot be copied without permission.

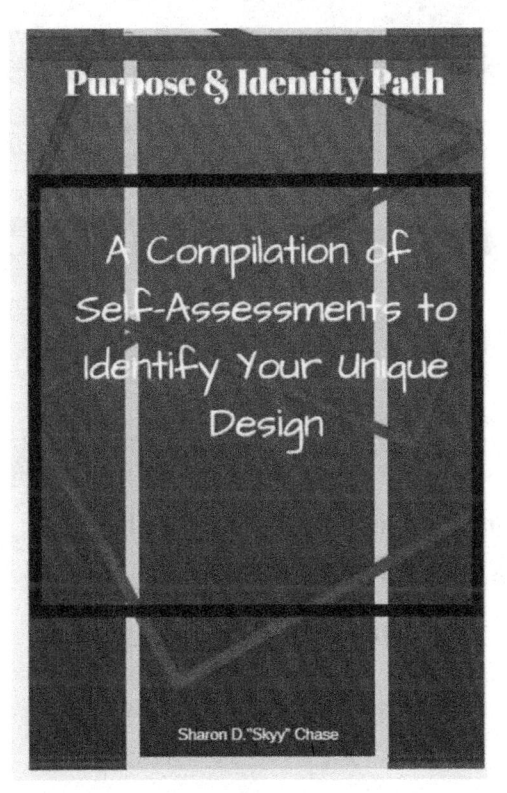

Purpose & Identity Path

A Compilation of Self-Assessments to Identify Your Unique Design

Sharon D. "Skyy" Chase

This program is a self-assessment that will take you on a deep dive of introspection to uncover your purpose. ™

COMPANY OF MEN ™

Book Review Club

Sharon D. "Skyy" Chase

This book club is exclusively for men of all ages & colors to dispel the myth that men don't read. To join send your email to info@skyychase.com

S.T.E.P.S.™

Strategies To Elevate You Out of Poverty Successfully

FINANCIAL FREEDOM GOALS

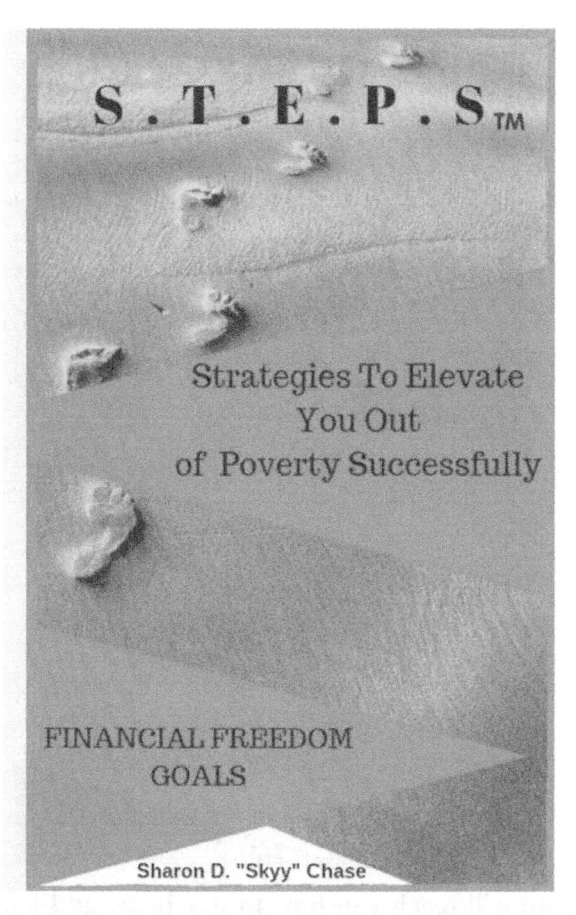

Sharon D. "Skyy" Chase

12 Steps Program to help you achieve your financial goals. In order to be successful, you must set financial goals; this program will set money goals that you can achieve with ease.

POSSESS YOUR™

G. IFTS
A. BILITIES
T. ALENTS
E. XPERTISE
S. KILLS

Sharon D. "Skyy" Chase

This program will teach you how to maximize and monetize your gifts, discover your talents, and make money utilizing all of your abilities. This is one of the most sought-after programs because a convergence and explosion will take place in your life and your finances.

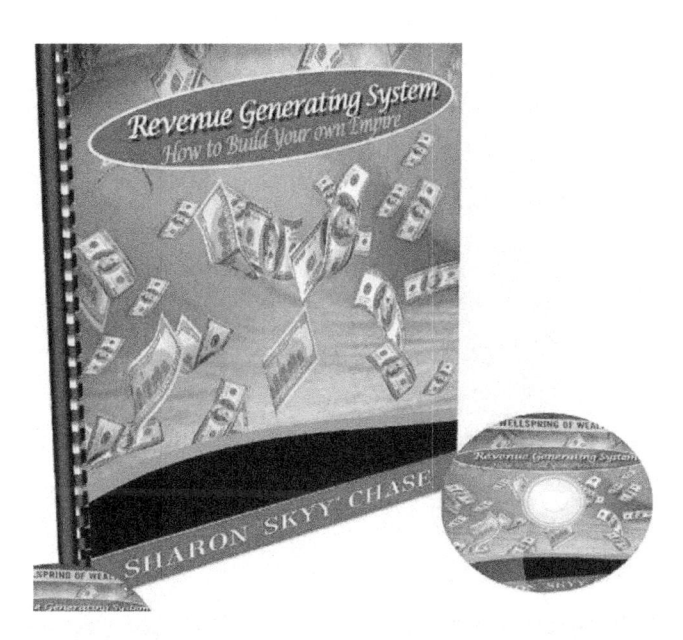

4 – week workshop teaching you How to build systems and processes to automate your business and make money while you sleep. ™

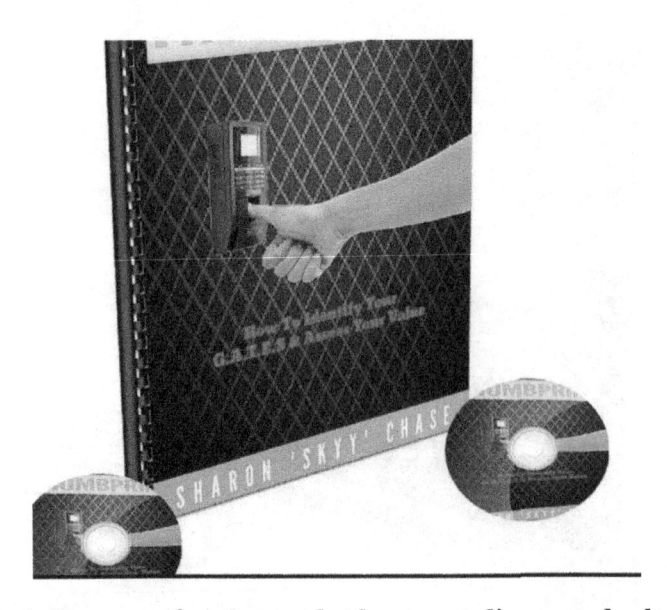

4 – Week Program for those who have not discovered what their talents are, this course will do a deep dive into five areas, what I termed G.A.T.E.S to utilize monetization in those key areas. ™

This workbook will give you the blueprint I used to write my book in five days. eBooks, all of the instructions are contained in this Million Dollar course. ©

Distinct™ Signature

Step - by - Step Credit Renewal Kit

Restore Your Good Name

This book will show you How to Restore your Good name and value in your signature. This kit contains 25 Letters of Dispute and 5 bonus scripts, giving you what to say and How to deal with collection agency calls.

Dear Mr. President -DOCUMENTARY COMING SOON 2019

An inside look at how the policies passed by the government affect the poor population in America. The government spends millions of dollars to fight the War on Poverty, it's time to fight that war from the inside out.

Join Me in
Eradicating
Annihilating
Erasing Poverty
Once and for All

Donations contact: info@skyychase.com

For every person that purchase my books or programs – I have created a program called PTC™ with me –Personal Touch Coaching™ Session with me valued at ($500.00) 30-minute session to show my appreciation for purchasing my products. Send your email to info@skyychase.com to schedule a session.

Have you ever paid for a coaching program and received only videos, with no contact with the Coach? I am concerned about your destiny, so I make myself available to anyone who purchases any of my products, not just my clients. You are spending your hard-earned money to invest in yourself and I want you to get 100% return on your investment. Thank you in advance.

Resources for Entrepreneurs
Business Start-up Checklist

You've decided to start a business. This is both an exciting and demanding time. The checklist below is meant to help new business owners by providing a list of the most common start-up steps. Depending on your particular industry, additional steps may be required for your particular business. I have provided this checklist to save you time.

Therefore, this checklist begins with incorporation. You will need to consult a lawyer, this just serves as a comprehensive list of things you will need to start.

- ✓ Incorporate your business or form your LLC with the state. Forming a business as a corporation or LLC helps to protect the owners' personal assets from the debts and liabilities of the business. There are also other advantages of forming a corporation or LLC, including certain tax advantages and establishing credibility for your new business with potential customers, vendor, employees, and partners.
- ✓ Prepare a business plan, if you have not done so already. Business plans define the Who, What, When, Where, and How your business and the products and/or services you plan to

provide. Business plans clearly outline the goals of the business, explain the operating procedures, detail the competition, include a marketing plan and explain the company's current and desired funding. If your company plans to seek funding either in the form of a traditional loan or from venture capitalists, a thorough business plan will be required for the application process.

✓ Select an accountant and attorney. Many small business owners turn to accountants and attorneys for advice when starting out, as well as through the life of the business. Many people seek referrals from friends, family members, or other small business owners in order to find an attorney and/or accountant. You may want to search for professionals who have worked with other small business owners, possibly in your same industry, and are familiar with the unique business situations small business owners often face.

✓ Obtain the federal tax identification number (also called employer identification number or EIN) for your business from the Internal Revenue Service (IRS). The EIN is like a social security number for a business and is required for corporations and LLCs that will have employees. The IRS uses this number to identify your business for all taxation matters. Business Filings can assist you with the preparation of IRS Form SS-4 for you to obtain an EIN or can obtain the EIN on behalf of your business.

✓ Obtain the state tax identification number for your business (if applicable). Some states require businesses to also have a state tax identification number. To learn if your state has this requirement, contact your state's taxation department.

- ✓ Open a business bank account. It is very important for corporations and LLCs to keep the finances of the business separate from those of the owners. To open a business bank account, most banks require information on the company, such as its formation date and type of business, and names and addresses of its owners. Some banks require corporations to provide a resolution from the board of directors or LLC members/managers authorizing the opening of the business bank account. In New York, a corporate or LLC seal is often required. It is advisable to contact the bank about their business bank account requirements prior to trying to open an account. That way, you will come prepared with all the necessary items.
- ✓ Apply for business loans (if applicable). Not all small business owners have enough of their own capital to start a business, and many seek outside funding from sources such as banks or through Small Business Administration (SBA) loan programs.
- ✓ Obtain the necessary business licenses and/or permits. Most businesses need licenses in order to begin operations. Licenses may be required for your city, your municipality, your county and/or your state. It is best to contact both your Secretary of State to check on business license requirements for your particular type of business and industry, and also to contact your local government agency in charge of licensing to learn their requirements and how to obtain the necessary licenses.
- ✓ Obtain business insurance. Just as you have personal insurance you should obtain insurance for your business. Some industries may have specific insurance requirements. Discuss your

particular industry and business needs with your insurance agent, to ensure you obtain the appropriate type and amount of insurance.

✓ Investigate other insurance and government requirements. Businesses face a number of government and insurance requirements, particularly if the business has employees. You should investigate your business's obligations for the following:

Unemployment insurance •
Workers' compensation •
OSHA requirements •
Federal tax •
State and local tax •
Self-employment tax •
Payroll tax requirements (such as FICA, federal unemployment tax, and state unemployment tax) •
Sales and use tax •

✓ Check zoning requirements. This is particularly important if you are starting a home-based business. You'll want to ensure you are meeting your city's zoning requirements for your area.

✓ Lease office space. If you are not going to be operating a home-based business, you'll probably need to find office space for your new company. Along with leasing an office, don't forget to purchase or lease the furniture and office equipment you will need to get your business up and running. This optional, in the age of social media most businesses, are started online, and office is utilized for event, workshops, seminars, although most business can be done strictly online.

98

- ✓ Set up your business accounting. You may decide that your accountant will handle the accounting for your business, or you may want to handle the accounting yourself with a small business accounting solution such as QuickBooks. Either way, you'll want to ensure that you are prepared to properly account for all business disbursements, payments received, invoices, accounts receivable/accounts payable, etc. Eventually, you will need an accountant, for copyright, trademark and tax purposes.
- ✓ Establish a line of credit for your business. Establishing a line of credit will help lessen the number of times your new business will be required to prepay for the products and services it purchases. It also helps establish a favorable credit history, which is helpful as your business begins establishing vendor and supplier relationships. As a subset of this, obtaining a D&B D.U.N.S. number for your business is also advisable. D&B (formerly Dun &Bradstreet) is the resource most often used to check the creditworthiness of a business. Structuring your business is critical in the beginning stages, this step allows you to do B2B and obtain government contracts, this is a stream of revenue that is overlooked by most entrepreneurs. In the age of internet and quick money, establishing a real business will allow you to make real money, one government contract can be worth millions.
- ✓ Create business materials. Having materials such as a logo for your business, business cards, and stationery will help your business develop an identity and potential customers find you.
- ✓ Develop a marketing plan for your products/services. A

primary reason you are starting your own business may be the hope of making money. In order to make sales, people need to be aware of what you're selling and how to find you.

SBA – Small Business Administration

The SBA provides a wealth of information and resources for small business owners.

SCORE

When starting a business most people are on a tight budget. Score is a group of retired professionals that serve as mentors to answers questions, unlike a coach; they will only provide limited service.

U.S Department of Labor

A handbook of statue and regulations administered by the Department of Labor.

This is just a small list of help that is available for startup entrepreneurs. For those interested in working with ACE I provide many services and products to help your transition into starting your own business a smooth one.

Business Plan
Product/Service Creation
Debt Repair
Certifications

It has been my pleasure to share my testimony and my journey with you. I wrote this book to inspire, motivate, uplift and elevate. Life is not a marathon but a journey; it is not given to the swift, but to the one who endures to the end.

About the Author

Sharon D. "Skyy" Chase is the owner of A.C.E Academy of Coaching/Consulting Excellence, LLC. & her non-profit Greater Works Global. As an entrepreneur, this is her dream to offer empowerment, education to emerging start-ups to help them utilize their God-given talent and step into purpose. Over the span of her career, she has helped hundreds of people achieve their lifelong goals. She holds a Bachelor's in Business, specializing in Finance. She teaches the 3M's of Money - How to Make, Multiply, and Manage your Money to fund your dream and leave a legacy. She is the mother of four and resides in Houston, Texas.

Bibliography-Work Cited Credits

Baskar, Mama. "The Complete Story of How Diamonds Are Mined." Business Insider. Business
  Insider, Inc, 06 Aug. 2012. Web. 07 Dec. 2015.

Grid Neff, Ilya. "Smugglers Defy Conflict-Diamonds Ban in Central African Republic." Bloomberg.com.
  Bloomberg, 22 Mar. 2015. Web. 08 Dec. 2015.

Hays, Jeffrey. "DIAMOND PROCESSING, CUTTING AND POLISHING." DIAMOND PROCESS0ING,
  CUTTING AND POLISHING. Nap, 2011. Web. 08 Dec. 2015.

989 International Interest Linkages and Monetary Policy. Basle, Switzerland: Bank for International Settlements.

1992a International Banking and Financial Market Developments. Basle, Switzerland: Bank for International Settlements.

The poverty guidelines may be formally referenced as "the poverty guidelines updated periodically in the Federal Register by the U.S. Department of Health and Human Services under the authority of 42 U.S.C. 9902(2)."

Made in the USA
Columbia, SC
13 November 2023